*Edward Thomas's Letters
to Jesse Berridge*

Jesse Berridge as a young man

The Letters of Edward Thomas to Jesse Berridge

with a memoir by Jesse Berridge

Edited and introduced by Anthony Berridge

LONDON
THE ENITHARMON PRESS
1983

ISBN 0905289 38 2

First published in 1983 by the Enitharmon Press
22 Huntingdon Road, East Finchley, London N2 9DU

Edward Thomas's letters © Myfanwy Thomas 1983
Jesse Berridge's memoir © Wilfrid Berridge 1983
Introduction, Epilogue and Notes © Anthony Berridge 1983

The Enitharmon Press acknowledges financial assistance
from the Arts Council of Great Britain

Printed and made in Great Britain by
Daedalus Press Wisbech Cambridgeshire

Contents

Prefatory Note and Acknowledgments	9
Introduction	11
The Letters	19
Memoir of Edward Thomas	84
Epilogue	91

Illustrations

Jesse Berridge as a young man	frontispiece
Facsimile of Edward Thomas's letter of 14 August 1902	31
Edward Thomas in 1904	43
All Saints' Vicarage, Witham	61
Jesse Berridge's house in Elsenham Street, Southfields, London	61
Edward Thomas about 1913	68
The Thomases' house on Bearsted Green	75
No 2 Yew Tree Cottages, Steep	75
Edward Thomas in uniform of the Artists' Rifles	81
Jesse Berridge about 1918	87
Jesse Berridge in later life	93

PHILIP EDWARD THOMAS
3 March 1878–9 April 1917

JESSE BERRIDGE
4 April 1874–4 February 1966

One thing I know, that love with chance
And use and time and necessity
Will grow, and louder the heart's dance
At parting than at meeting be.
      EDWARD THOMAS *Collected Poems*

Prefatory Note and Acknowledgments

'It is to the credit of Thomas's friends that his letters have not been sold, but I hope they will not remain unpublished' declared the late Judge Eckert in 1937, in the introduction to his biography of Edward Thomas. Since then, a good number of the letters have indeed been published (and, one must regretfully add, not a few have been sold). Extracts from Thomas's letters to his friend Jesse Berridge first appeared in John Moore's *Life and Letters of Edward Thomas* in 1939 and they have been quoted from in several more recent publications. None, however, has hitherto been printed in full. The collection in this volume is the first that can claim to be complete in every respect; all the letters known to have been written by Thomas to Berridge are included, and no word or sentence has been omitted. Grateful acknowledgment is due to Mr Wilfrid Berridge, their owner, for giving his consent to the publication of Edward Thomas's letters to his father and for the use of unpublished photographs, and to the National Library of Wales for permission to print Letter 63 which is in their possession. I would also like to thank the copyright holder Mrs Myfanwy Thomas for permission to print copyright material (by her mother as well as her father) and for authorising the reproduction of previously unpublished photographs of Edward Thomas, for which acknowledgments are also due to the Bodleian Library, the Imperial War Museum and the National Portrait Gallery. Acknowledgment is due to the Oxford University Press for quotation from a poem by Edward Thomas.

I think I should confess that my interest in the letters arose not only from a devotee's desire to read everything that Edward Thomas wrote but also out of my curiosity about his correspondent, my namesake. It seemed possible that Jesse Berridge had been a cousin of my father's; they had been almost exact contemporaries; both of them had family roots in Leicestershire and became canons of the Church of England. My hopes were disappointed; if there was a family connection it must have been several generations ago. However my correspondence with Canon Jesse's son had a happy outcome in that it led to his generous offer to lend me the letters with a view to my typing and editing them for publication. This book is the result.

In my work on the notes and background to the letters, I have received valuable help not only from Wilfrid Berridge and Myfanwy Thomas (both of whom gave me much personal encouragement) but also from Canon Berridge's sister-in-law, Mrs Phyllis Berridge, from Mr Ron Warsup, Lady Williams, Mr Meirion Griffith and Mrs Joan Stevens. Mrs Rowland Watson kindly let me see her late husband's copy of Berridge's memoir of his friend, so that I have been able to restore some passages missing from the original manuscript. I am also grateful to Mr A. C. Edwards and the editor of the *Essex Journal* for allowing me to reprint part of an obituary of Jesse Berridge, to the archivists of King's College, London and of the City of London School, to the Librarian of Lincoln College, Oxford, and to Dr R. George Thomas, whose edition of Edward Thomas's letters to Gordon Bottomley has proved to be a model of scholarly editing which I could not live up to and an indispensable source of cross-references in my own research.

To readers already familiar with the story of Edward Thomas's life the biographical summary in my Introduction may seem superfluous, if not presumptuous, but I hope it will be helpful to newcomers to Thomas and lead them to discover his prose works and poetry for themselves. I have included a somewhat fuller account of the life and background of Jesse Berridge, partly because he is probably the least known of Edward Thomas's regular correspondents (who now proves to have been a remarkable person in his own right) but also because I believe that Thomas himself would have wished this record of their friendship to be as far as possible worthy of them both.

Thomas's addresses, dates, signatures, abbreviations and punctuation are printed as he wrote them. Words which he underlined have been italicised, as have titles of publications and quotations in foreign languages. To the very few undated letters I have added in square brackets the actual or approximate date. A chronological list of the works of Edward Thomas referred to in the letters and notes can be found at the end of the book.

ANTHONY BERRIDGE

Introduction

In 1901, when he first met and started to exchange letters with Jesse Berridge, Edward Thomas was twenty-three years old. He had been down from Oxford for a year, and was making a bare living by reviewing books for the *Daily Chronicle* (though not yet regularly) and by occasional success in placing his essays and imaginative sketches in a variety of periodicals. He had recently installed himself, his wife, and their sixteen-month-old son in rooms above a Balham laundry office. The rent, ten shillings a week, was more than his uncertain income could meet and he was having to sell most of the books he had acquired at university. Before the end of the year Edward, Helen and Mervyn Thomas would be moving out of London for good, to the first of their seven homes in the country.

Jesse Berridge was twenty-seven. Within six years he would be an Anglican priest, but at this time he was still a clerk in a City bank, as he had been since leaving school at the age of fifteen. He had been married for six years; like the Thomases, Jesse and Edna Berridge had one son and were living frugally in rented rooms in West London. They too would shortly be moving, to a newly-developed area of Wandsworth. Whilst Thomas spent his spare time walking over countryside and commons, Berridge devoted his to sketching and sculpting, to reading philosophy and writing romantic sonnets.

It was at the home of Berridge's friend T. C. Williams that the two men came to know each other. Duncan Williams, as he was always called, was a twenty-nine-year-old clerk employed by the London County Council. He lived on the top floor of Clovelly (now Dulverton) Mansions, an imposing new block of flats in Gray's Inn Road. His family came from North Wales and (unlike Thomas) he spoke Welsh; since he also collected folk-songs, read widely and enjoyed the open air his company must have been very congenial to Thomas. He later became a frequent visitor to the Thomases at Elses Farm and at Steep (where he took some of the best-known and first-published photographs of Edward Thomas in 1913). Soon after his friend's death, Williams wrote an appreciation for the little magazine *Today*. He mourns his 'elusive personality' and recalls how he and Thomas used to spend 'the day in fishing or sauntering, and the evening in talk, fetch the supper beer in a jug from the inn up the lane, introduce or learn some newly discovered old song of the English or the Welsh folk, and sometimes set off after dark for an all-night tramp.'

Edward Thomas probably first met Duncan Williams through his wife Helen's old Hammersmith friends, the actor Franklin Dyall and the poet Charles Dalmon, who were sharing rooms in Gray's Inn Road at the time; they had been part of the mildly bohemian circle which Helen joined when she lived at Beatrice Logan's house in St Peter's Square while Edward was at Oxford. It seems likely that Berridge too was introduced to these friends by his wife, since Edna, a professional artist and herself something of a bohemian, was living with a married sister in neighbouring Chiswick when she met her future husband. Many years later, Berridge thought he might have first met Duncan Williams at Kelmscott House. Certainly, all these friends shared an interest in the ideas of William Morris, who had died in 1896.

That Edward Thomas and Jesse Berridge so quickly became close friends is not surprising when one considers the similarity of their circumstances. Both had married young (at the age of twenty-one) against the wishes of their more conventional parents, and had kept their marriages secret, from fellow-students at Oxford and from colleagues at the bank; each was living in rented rooms in one of the new London suburbs, and had a young son as well as a wife to support on a meagre income; each was engaged in writing (though only one of them was trying to make a living from it) and would in fact have a book published in the following year. Even in appearance they were alike; Thomas was taller, but both were strongly-built, fair, and strikingly good-looking.

Jesse Berridge may already have been considering the possibility of ordination. In 1904 he was in charge of the Ferndale Mission in the Royal Albert Docks, and in January of that year he enrolled himself as an evening student at King's College, London, to prepare for the Associateship which would qualify him for the Anglican priesthood. Ordinands were required to spend two years at evening and a third at morning classes, taking Latin, Greek and Hebrew, as well as Theology and Music. So Berridge left the City for good in 1905. In the following year he passed his finals with first class honours. He also achieved some literary success at King's : he contributed several prose pieces to the college *Review*, and won the Carter Prize for English two years running with verses on the set subjects of 'The Death of Nelson' and 'The Strand'. While living in Southfields the family had increased by two sons; in the summer of 1905 they moved to East Ham for a few months and there the last child, Wilfrid, was born.

In 1906 Berridge was ordained deacon in the diocese of St Alban's, which covered the whole of Essex until the diocese of Chelmsford was founded in 1914. After a short period as curate of Holy Trinity, Harrow Green, he spent two years at St Botolph's, Colchester, during which time he was ordained priest. After this he was curate in charge of All Saints, Witham (1908-10), St Luke's, Leyton (1910-12), and Wanstead (1912-15); during his last curacy he also acted as chaplain to the Hackney Infant Orphan Asylum. In 1915 he spent the year as chaplain of the Essex County Asylum at Brentwood, living in Rose Valley in the town, but he had not been there long before he was appointed to the living of Little Baddow, near Chelmsford. In the following spring he moved his family into the rectory which he was to occupy for over thirty years.

The correspondence starts on a somewhat enigmatic note of protest from Edward Thomas. The most probable explanation seems to be that Berridge had written to Irene MacArthur, Helen Thomas's married elder sister, in jest or reproach on the subject of her passion for the French actress Sarah Bernhardt. Edmond Rostand's new play *L'Aiglon* was shortly to be presented at Her Majesty's Theatre after its wildly successful opening in Paris the previous year and a short season in New York in April 1901. The title was Victor Hugo's nickname for Napoleon's son and heir, the Duc de Reichstadt, an ineffectual 'young eagle' who died in 1833 at the age of twenty-one. The part was played by Bernhardt herself though she was by then in her late fifties. Irene MacArthur admired her intensely; she made herself known to her and visited her at her holiday retreat on Belle Isle.

Be that as it may, any hard feelings aroused by whatever Berridge had written to Thomas's sister-in-law were soon forgotten. With the eagerness and social assurance that still remained with him from his undergraduate days, Thomas plied his new acquaintance with brief but persuasive notes suggesting further meetings, and Berridge was evidently responsive. Within a year, Thomas's notes have become intimate full-length letters in which one can sense his relief at the opportunity to share and clarify his feelings about whatever was preoccupying him at the time. Though it must have helped a little to reduce the loneliness and uncertainty that increasingly assailed him, correspondence with a growing number of friends was never a satisfactory substitute for the delight he found in their company and conversation. He needed their presence. As Berridge remarks in his Memoir, almost every letter he received from Thomas contains a suggestion or confirmation of a visit or a meeting in London or a walk in the country or a cycling holiday. The London meetings did not have to be prearranged, since until 1905 Berridge could be found at the bank any day and from that year onwards Thomas was sure to be at the St George's restaurant in St Martin's Lane on alternate Wednesdays, talking with fellow-writers over a late tea; this may explain some of the long intervals between letters in certain years of the correspondence. Jesse Berridge was the first of the lifelong intimate friends whom Edward Thomas made after leaving Oxford; he was one of the small number whose friendship in these early years (in the words of John Moore) 'so warmed and cheered him that even in his blackest moods it could make him believe that, after all, the world was good and that he shared a little in its goodness'.

Whether Berridge unburdened himself in letters of equal frankness we shall never know, though we gather that he was the less fluent and assiduous correspondent of the two. Not one of his letters to Edward Thomas has survived; any that may originally have been preserved would have been destroyed in the bonfire which Thomas made of his papers while on leave from the army in summer 1916, preparing for the last of many domestic upheavals, the move from Steep to High Beech. However, what does survive in Berridge's own hand more than compensates for the loss of his letters. In 1946 Rowland Watson, secretary of the Edward Thomas Memorial Committee, invited a number of Thomas's friends, as well as his children and brothers, to contribute to a volume of reminiscences of him. The response was magnificent, but Watson was unsuccessful in finding a publisher and the project was abandoned. Jesse Berridge's contribution, of which he kept a copy, is now printed for the first time. He would surely have been glad that this Memoir should be published with the letters which he so carefully preserved, for they complement each other to present a fresh portrait of Edward Thomas and a moving record of 'the momentous experience of his friendship'.

Philip Edward Thomas was born in Lambeth on 3 March 1878, the eldest of the six sons of Philip Henry and Mary Elizabeth Thomas. Both his parents had been born and brought up in Monmouthshire. His father was a civil servant in the Board of Trade; he was later described by his eldest son as 'eloquent, confident, black-haired, brown-eyed, all that my mother was not'. There was a bond of affection between Edward and his mother that was unique in the family and remained strong to the end; he certainly inherited her diffidence and her often melancholy temperament, as well as her beautiful features and voice.

In Edward's second year the Thomases moved to Wakehurst Road, close to Wandsworth Common, and when he was eleven to Shelgate Road, which is near Clapham Common. They were not a happy family: 'the best of life was passed out of the home and out of school,' Edward recalled, and he and his friends made the most of the labyrinth of new streets and the still unspoilt commons of south London for their games and explorations. The Thomas boys also had opportunities for adventure further afield when they were sent on holiday to relatives in Somerset, Wiltshire and South Wales. Edward was indifferent to cricket and football, but he could outwalk any boy of his age and covered the three miles to Wimbledon Common when he was nine. Richmond Park and its wildlife were soon within his range. Like many other boys he went fishing, kept rabbits and pigeons, collected butterflies and birds' eggs, but in Edward the hobbies developed very early into a deep love and expert knowledge of natural history. He kept detailed notes of his observations of birds, trees and flowers, and was having articles printed by the time he was seventeen.

There were several changes of school, Mr Thomas rarely being satisfied with any for long. Edward was finally sent to St Paul's in Hammersmith to prepare for university. After four rather unhappy terms he failed to win a scholarship to Balliol but went up to Oxford all the same, living as a non-collegiate student at lodgings in the Cowley Road. He then won a history scholarship to Lincoln, moved into college, and duly took his degree at the end of his third year. He had read at least as widely in literature as in history and had a good knowledge of Latin, Greek, French and German. In 1899 he had married Helen Noble; she was the second daughter of James Ashcroft Noble, the eminent critic who had earlier encouraged Edward to publish his first book, *The Woodland Life*. Mervyn was born the following year, before his father had left Oxford.

Rather than enter the civil service as his father wished, Edward was determined to live by his pen. In the next fifteen years it proved to be a precarious living for himself and Helen and their three children. From November 1902 he was a regular reviewer of books for the *Daily Chronicle* and later for the *Morning Post*, and he contributed as a free-lance to a variety of periodicals. He was commissioned to write literary biographies (notably of Jefferies, Swinburne, Borrow and Pater) and introductions to pocket editions of various classics of English literature. He wrote topographical texts to accompany the illustrations of artists better paid than himself. More to his own satisfaction but even less lucratively, he published collections of his contemplative essays and dream-like prose idylls, a semi-autobiographical novel (*The Happy-Go-Lucky Morgans*), and an account of his childhood; he also produced several anthologies. It was a drudgery which he could only escape by going off to visit his friends or on long walks and cycling tours. (Few people can have known the southern counties of England and Wales as intimately as Edward Thomas came to know them in those pre-war years.) Even his journeys had to be turned to good account, but the books which resulted, such as *Beautiful Wales, The South Country* and *In Pursuit of Spring*, were written from the heart.

The family seemed to be constantly on the move. For a year after Oxford they endured dismal lodgings in Earlsfield and Balham. In September 1901, soon after the first meeting with Jesse Berridge, they moved to Kent: first to Rose Acre Cottage outside Bearsted, then to a house on the village green (1903-4), then to Elses Farm near Sevenoaks (1904-6). They moved to Hampshire so that Mervyn could attend Bedales School daily, living at Berryfield Cottage, Ashford (1906-9), Wick Green (1909-13) and No 2 Yew Tree Cottages in Steep (1913-16). Their last home together was at High Beech in Epping Forest. Bronwen was born at Bearsted in 1902, Myfanwy at Wick Green in 1910. It fell to Helen to hold the family together through the fluctuations in Edward's fortune, health and moods. 'She loved defeating poverty by providing ample dishes out of nothing, she rejoiced in her strong health that could carry all loads,' wrote Eleanor Farjeon. Helen's own joyful and heart-rending account of her life with Edward, in *As It Was* and *World Without End*, has long been recognised as a masterpiece in its own right.

As Jesse Berridge reminds us in his Memoir, the story is not one of unrelieved hardship and gloom; there were treats and laughter and much hospitality as well. But self-doubt seems to have been deeply rooted in Thomas and it surfaced, in his early thirties, in bouts of increasingly severe depression, intensified by financial worries and by sheer exhaustion. It has been estimated that he reviewed some twelve hundred books; he also wrote or compiled more than thirty of his own, half of which appeared between 1909 and 1912. His health was already causing serious concern in 1908 and three years later it broke down completely. A long period in Wales helped to restore it and two new friendships – Eleanor Farjeon's from 1912 and Robert Frost's from 1913 – seem finally to have relieved his sense of isolation. The arrival of Frost was momentous, for it was he who persuaded Thomas to see himself as a poet and gave him the confidence to prove that he was.

When he started writing in verse in December 1914 Thomas had established a reputation as a distinguished critic and a master of English prose, but he himself estimated the public which knew him as a reviewer, essayist and biographer as numbering no more than two thousand. He had been writing for this public for twelve years. His entire poetic output, which was to bring him fame (posthumously) on a far wider scale, was achieved in the following twenty-five months.

Since August 1914 Great Britain had been at war with Germany. In July 1915 Thomas abandoned his plan to visit the Frosts in America and enlisted in the Artists' Rifles. He was sent to teach map-reading at a camp near Romford. His health and his spirits quickly improved: to the bewilderment of his friends he appeared, outwardly, to have become a different man. In November 1916 he was commissioned as an artillery officer and volunteered for service abroad. He embarked for Le Havre at the end of January 1917. Little of the poetry which he had imperturbably continued writing during the eighteen months in uniform refers directly to the war, and he wrote none in France. Edward Thomas's collected poems number one hundred and forty-four. He did not live to see more than a dozen of them in print, nor any over his own name, for early on the morning of Easter Monday, 9 April 1917, at the beginning of the Battle of Arras, he was killed by the blast from a shell. It was just five weeks since his thirty-ninth birthday.

His old paper, the *Daily Chronicle*, paid tribute to 'a writer of wonderful charm, a man of rare personality; preserving a quite boyish heart with the wisdom and gentle balance of years. Whether his subject chanced to be George Borrow or Swinburne, lyric form or the Sussex Downs, the style was the man'. Today we may feel that we come even closer to Edward Thomas the man in his poems and in his letters. In 1917 his poetic genius had yet to be recognised. Later still, the gradual publication of his letters (and the reminiscences of his contemporaries) confirmed that he had no less remarkable a gift for friendship. As Helen Thomas reflected in a letter to Janet Hooton in May 1917, his friends were of all kinds: 'men and women, great and small, rich and poor, clever and simple, they loved him as very few men are loved'. The words which Robert Frost wrote to Helen soon after Edward's death must have expressed the feelings of them all: 'he was the bravest and best and dearest man you and I have ever known.'

[1]

                              7 Nightingale Parade,
                              Balham, S.W.
                              31. v. 1901

My dear Berridge,

    Will you come and see us on Tuesday or Wednesday next? Baby and Mrs Thomas join in the wish to see you, and I think they would like to have Mrs and Master Berridge, too.

    A letter is more convenient than conversation for mentioning a rather nasty subject. Irene tells everyone everything, as you know, & I have just heard of your letter to her about 'L'Aiglon.' I cannot help mentioning this, partly because I hope we may be friends some day, & therefore, not wanting to be in the dark, I am curious as to your motive; partly because I don't like to think that Irene's friends will make her suffer for her childish, impetuous mistakes. Do you understand? Or do I speak with tongues?

    I shall be in tomorrow evening after half past six if you care to call.

    Yours very sincerely
            Edward Thomas

Please remember me to Mrs Berridge.

Master Berridge was Jesse Dell, aged five at this time. Irene MacArthur was Helen Thomas's sister. 'L'Aiglon': poetic drama by Edmond Rostand, 1900. (v. Introduction p. 13).

[2]

                              7 Nightingale Parade,
                              Balham, S.W.
                              25. vi. 01.

My dear Berridge,

    When are you coming to see me again? or when may I come to see you? At present I have no engagements except for Saturday. My conscience is just beginning to talk about a cigarette case which has been in my study for a long time & turns out to be yours. As for the Greek play, it seems to me to be melodrama, full of comic & not tragic irony, and I have burned it. If you know what it was like, you would not think me unkind in doing so.

By the way, would you be too tired – some evening this week – to walk 3 or 4 miles with me to an old resort of mine that used to be a sweet place, known to the world as Merton? Perhaps you don't know just the part I mean: I have known it for fifteen years, & should be very glad to revisit the place with you.
Ever yours
      Edward Thomas

[3]

Rose Acre,
Bearsted,
nr Maidstone
18. xii. 1901

My dear Berridge,

Can you all come & see us here on Saturday? There is a 5/- week-end ticket from Victoria to Maidstone. Bearsted is the next station, so you travel on & pay the difference of $2\frac{1}{2}$d. If you must return before Monday there is a train from here to Victoria at 8.4 p.m. There are several trains to Bearsted during the afternoon but I believe that one leaving Victoria at about 3 is the last for which cheap tickets are available. If you can't catch that, start from Holborn, whence you can travel by any train at same rate: you then stop at *West* Maidstone where I should meet you & walk the $2\frac{1}{4}$ miles to this house. We should all like to be remembered by Mrs. Berridge & the boy and by yourself.
Yours ever
      Edward Thomas

P.S. Let me know soon, & don't trouble to bring any luggage. *I* can lend *you* everything.

The move to Bearsted took place in September. Of all the houses from which these letters were written, only Rose Acre Cottage, which was a mile from the village, no longer stands.

[4]

Rose Acre,
Bearsted,
nr Maidstone
24. xii. 1901

My dear Berridge,

I am very sorry you couldn't come. I should, I think, have been able to give you some delightful hours, & you no less would have made me rejoice in the beauty of this land. I can now only send you & Mrs. Berridge & the boy our best wishes. For in my present anxious circumstances I cannot without the inspiration of your presence say a single cheerful thing, & cannot therefore write a letter. When you feel able to come let me know & if I am free I shall be happy to welcome you here. If it is fine weather then, *il faut cultiver notre jardin.* I find in gardening the properties of Lethe & of Styx.

Ever yours
   Edward Thomas

[5]
         Rose Acre,
         Bearsted,
         nr Maidstone
         14. i. 1902

My dear Berridge,

I will begin by saying, what my whole letter should say, that I was as happy to have your letter as you would have had me be. It was particularly delightful to know that you have kept a mental diary for me – as I have for you. No doubt it has been recorded in some commonplace book in the skies, which we shall some day enjoy. But I hope we shall meet many times before then, & as to a visit in February let it be early & long. If possible write and suggest a day now, lest I should have to disappoint you. I think I said that the cheap ticket takes you to Maidstone & that you go on to Bearsted & pay the difference at the end.

I am glad you have met G.K.C. I admire some of his verse & his prose very much. I think he is a big man, & wonder what his entirely mature work will be. Oldershaw was in the History form at St. Paul's with me, but he was several years older & I only once met him at Oxford. He will remember me as a coy & foolish boy. Is Masterman the author of *Folia Dispersa* a recent book of verse? I reviewed him in the *Chronicle*, perhaps too flippantly, though I couldn't hide my liking for his best work. He was a stranger to me.

I shall be an early reader of your book when it appears. As a rule my friends' books are a great surprise. I thought I knew them so well & was amazed to find that I did not know them at all. Of your work I know nothing at first hand, & yet I flatter myself that I shall recognise it when I see it. You will no doubt feel some dissatisfaction if your early book is published. The question is, I think, not 'have I outgrown it?', but 'did it really portray or delicately suggest a self that has passed away?' I think I have a right to ridicule my own first book because it is a mere anatomy of myself & my emotions when I was 17. So much is that true, that I often find myself now trying in my essays to gather up the drift from that far-off time.

I have lately been fairly busy (not in work which pays, but in mere practice essays which will never be printed). Perhaps I will show you some of the knick-knacks when you come. I will, however, amuse you with a tour of their titles.

    (i)   Hengest: a Kentish study (an old gardener & idealist)
    (ii) The Most Beautiful House in the World.
    (iii) The Books of Restingham (an imaginary country house)
    (iv) On Being Extremely Digressive (self-castigating satire)
    (v) Cleopatra (the tragedy of a poor poet's cat).

Alas! they are all most unfilial to their titles – I have one secret – a few weeks ago I sent a volume of my essays to Duckworth, calling it *Horae Solitariae*. I have no guess whether it will be accepted. You will blame my only reason for sending it – it would be a good advertisement if well received. You see, I am at present very unsuccessful & unable to pay my way, & must do anything that will help to make a banking account. I can't live in the country very happily on credit, so there is no alternative. The worst of it is that I can't create a real pot-boiler. As a rule I can't get much nearer to a pot-boiler that I did in my "Isoud with the white hands." That paper has probably lit a pleasant fire by now; for the Editor to whom I sent it in October refuses to answer my request for news of it. I shall try the effect of a solicitor's letter to him, soon – for I have only a rough draft of it & I love it as a father loves his idiot child. I did delete the 'toast'. During my 4 months here I have sent papers to more than a dozen journals & magazines & have had about 40 refusals; one paper, e.g., I sent to 9 different editors. Perhaps then I am justified in deferring my 'magnificat.'

By the way, I want to read again Lowell's essays *From my Study Windows* and the *Biglow Papers*. I believe they are in the detestable 'Scott Library.' Will you get them for me? & I will pay by return – I haven't sufficient stamps to send, or I would.

Mervyn is very well now, after a cold caught in London at Christmas time. I hope the young Jesse is well; he ought to be at Bearsted, too. Remember us all to him & to Mrs. Berridge.

    Ever yours,
              Edward Thomas

Remember me to Duncan & Margaret when you see them – and to Simpson.

G. K. C: G. K. Chesterton, who was two years older than ET and left St. Paul's in 1892, four terms before ET joined the History VIII. Lucian Oldershaw was one of Chesterton's closest friends there, and later his wife's brother-in-law; he went up to Christ Church, Oxford, where he founded the undergraduate magazine JCR referred to in Letter 7. The author of Folia Dispersa was C. M. Masterman, poet and essayist, not C. F. G. Masterman, whom ET probably had in mind (see note to Letter 11). JB's book: The White Altar, a collection of sonnets (1902), dedicated to his wife. James Russell Lowell (1819-91) was an American essayist, poet and diplomat.

[6]

Rose Acre,
Bearsted,
nr Maidstone
16. i. 1902

My dear Berridge,

Thank you very much for your kindness & astonishing speed. I enclose &c – I expect you will write soon & so will I – For today I am busy with the poems of Mary Robinson (Madame Duclaux) & have a long night before me –

Ever yours
    Edward Thomas

ET's review appeared in the Daily Chronicle on 20.1.02.

[7]

[written on 2 sheets of LINCOLN COLLEGE, OXFORD headed paper]

Rose Acre
28. i. 1902

My dear Berridge,

For about a fortnight I have been changed into a business animal. I have been writing far too many letters for my purse to publishers & editors, and trying to make a new source of income. You have heard of Dent's venture – a magazine called *The Country*? I hoped to get a favoured place on it, but after a long correspondence, introductions &c, am merely promised that short articles from my pen will be considered. Dent is now considering my suggestion of a 3rd. volume of Lamb's essays in the Temple Classics. If he adopts it, I trust he will make me editor & in course of a few years pay me the consequent £5. You would laugh to see the list of subjects – from history to ornithology

('Truth & conchology') – which I sent to the Editor of a new Encyclopaedia as within my range. To eat & drink here I find I must go anhungered & athirst. I have also sent Blackwood's a long moonstruck paper called 'A Rosary of Evil Days' & it is being considered. So you are right in saying I am 'busy enough' but wrong in saying I am 'paid for my imaginings.' My imaginings all in a cupboard & only my lies in print.

Your letter was a great gift. But I can't tell you how much I lived in the ragged fancy of 'an old deserted Surrey manor house' & its garden which you told me of. I believe now that it was my fancy and not yours. In fact I put on paper – in fragments – some fragments – some memoranda of a fancy as like it as a replica to an original, two years ago. Your letter has set fire to the dim & smoky thing, & I shall very likely make a companion to 'Isoud' out of it. Do you mind such a malversation? 'The Books of Restingham' is a prosaic paper, containing extracts from Polydore Vergil, Quarles, Gesner's friend Caius, & woven together by a thin sketch of a foxhunting lord of the manor.

I am glad to hear even of Brimley Johnson's offer. Tell me when you have saved £9:10 & then . . . I should like to.

You don't say whether you have met Oldershaw. I knew him as an extremely gentle, bookish & clever big boy. He was a Fabian at Oxford. Nothing of his literary work ever struck me, – but I have seen little. He started an unusually good magazine at Oxford which I helped to its fate in '99.

Keep Hazlitt until you buy Dent's new edition, or always.

I must end in a hurry & therefore beg a letter from you *ut illa sanctificata sint.* With greetings to you all

Ever yours
   Edward Thomas

R. *Brimley Johnson published JB's second book,* Sonnets of a Platonist *(see letter 20).*

[8]
Rose Acre,
Bearsted,
nr Maidstone
12. iii. 1902

My dear Berridge,

I don't know whether to be glad or sorry that your silence had so good an excuse.But I am very sorry to hear that Mrs. Berridge & the boy have been ill. We sympathize very much though we can't conceive of illnesses here where we make as much of this fine weather as the crocuses the rooks & the willow trees. In a superior way of course – having one acre of our own – we congratulate you on your garden; we may even be able to help you, though our own experience has been slow & dearly bought. I only hope you haven't got a lot of new brick dust & mortar instead of loam to work upon. But in a London garden, there is one good rule: when in doubt, sow *sweet peas*. A penny packet will make a score of ladders as rich in dreams as Jacob's. I have unfortunately had to vary my gardening with selling my books. Until last week I had earned nothing for a long time & had to get nearly seventy pounds by selling books. Now I hope I may have peace for a while. But my peace of mind returns rather slowly & since I sent you my last letter I have written little – a paper on Collins & Quarles & some notes on a poacher &c. I make plans almost daily. I shall probably never execute more than half, & not more than one or two until I find that editors will read my work. One poor little paper of mine has been in vain to 16 editors in the past 4 months, yet when it appears in *Horae Solitariae* it will perhaps be praised. When that will be I can't say. Duckworth will probably take his time. But if it can be managed I want it to be out in May, because it will then have some sale at Oxford, where my friends will be spending their last term. 'Isoud' will be in it: a solicitor recovered it from the editor's maw. I fear the title of the book will be against it. It has come to mean too much to me, however, to be dropped now. *Horae Solitariae* you know is the one unread book in my shelves – unopened in fact. I am told it is theology. I keep it for its title & for its faintly shining old calf.

You mention 'The Octopus'. What is it? Who wrote it? I have never seen it or heard of it. I give you a counter question – have you read *Polyphemus & other Poems* by a man called Trevelyan (published by Brimley Johnson). I reviewed it & am still fond of it & I think you would like it much. And have you read *The Roadmender* (Duckworth 2/6)? The author was a woman who lately died, *aet* 33: read it if you have a chance. These facts are not generally known, & they ought to be, for the right understanding of the book which is exquisite minor prose.

I want to see you. When can you come? I think we shall be free for most of April, not before. We all want to be remembered by Mrs. Berridge & the boy.

Yours ever
    Edward Thomas

R. C. Trevelyan (1872-1951) later became a friend of ET's. The author of The Roadmender, *Margaret Fairless Barber (1869-1901), used the* pseudonym 'Michael Fairless'. ET described her as 'a gifted woman, lately deceased, drawing upon an experience which we can only know to have been tragically rich – she was a roadmender for half a year.' (Reviews in DC, 23.3.02 & 25.3.02).

[9]

Rose Acre,
Bearsted,
nr Maidstone
13. iv. 1902

My dear Berridge,

As you are coming on Saturday, I won't write. You had better take the 2.45 from Victoria (about same time at Holborn, I think). Take 5/- return to Maidstone East. Bearsted is the next station, & you pay the 3d. difference – the next train is about 4.10. For return, there is the 8.4 p.m. on Sunday & the 9.14 a.m. on Monday. Let me know when to expect you & tell Mrs. Berridge we shall be sorry not to see her & the boy.

Yours ever
Edward Thomas

P.S. In the 'Woodland Life' the 'naturalist' is a very mediocre one. Whether the style is good for a boy of 17 I can't say. But I am sorry Oldershaw [   ] I am a naturalist.
[*added at head of letter*]   Do send me your volume as soon as you can. I *may* never have it from the *Chronicle*.

Word missing in postscript, where the letter is damaged.

[10]

Rose Acre,
Bearsted,
27. iv. 02.

My dear Berridge,

I am tired out. I haven't been well, & now I have just had 24 hours furious work for the *Chronicle*. But I ought to have found time before to talk about *The White Altar*. Now I have time I simply can't. I like 'Te Deum' & several other lyrics. But the sonnets I cannot wholly understand. I like them, but they seem personal to such an extent that I cannot follow them: I haven't the clue: and so far I have not found in them that symbolism which the most purely personal verse sometimes has – e.g.

Shakespeare's. The great poet loses part of his passion by a kind of intellectuality. In your sonnets I see the passion & can only here & there discover the buried intellect. Perhaps you can help me out of the slough. Please try: "Not verse now, only prose." And put down my diabolical frankness to my exhaustion. As I said before, I am tired.
    Yours ever
        Edward Thomas

[11]

Rose Acre,
Bearsted,
nr Maidstone
May 3, 1902

My dear Berridge,

Did I talk about symbolism in my tired letter? Then I was a fool, at least if I blamed you for not being symbolic. What I meant was – that it was impossible for any outsider to understand you fully. That I thought was a weakness. Perhaps on a second reading I shall change my mind. I can't say now, because I am worn out by rapid and very uncongenial work; and now I have 40 pages of proofs to correct. *Horae Solitariae* is to be called *Horae Solitariae* after all. My worst things, I find, come first. The book is no secret. I shall be happy if you tell everybody about it, especially if they may buy it. As you know, I am forced to depend entirely on that kind of advertisement. It should be out on May 30.

I may be in Oxford, next Friday. If I am free at all I should like to meet you there or walk out to Tiddington – would you mind making a suggestion? I will do my best to fall in with it. My address at Oxford will be:
        c/o A. A. Stanford Esqre.,
          Lincoln College,
          Oxford.
Write there after Wednesday, unless you hear from me before.

When is your book to appear? I haven't had it or any other verse, since February.

Many thanks –

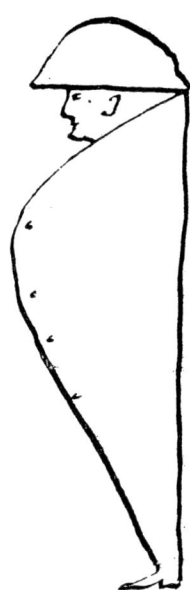

this is a Napoleon Buonaparte for Mervyn, not for you – many thanks for the 'Patriots' Club' paper. How much does it cost to become a patriot? And do they accept sleepy rustic members?

With kindest regards to Mrs. Berridge, your mother & the boys,
　Ever yours
　　　　Edward

The ink drawing is repeated at the end of the letter. JB's mother was living at Rose Cottage, Tiddington. Archibald Ambrose Stanford was 22 at this time; he lived in Dublin, and entered the College from Marlborough the year after ET. The papers of the Patriots' Club were edited by Lucian Oldershaw and published in 1904 under the title England; a Nation. *G. K. Chesterton and C. F. G. Masterman were contributors.*

[12]

　　　　　　　　　　　　　　　　Rose　Acre
　　　　　　　　　　　　　　　　6. v. 1902

My dear Berridge,

I quite forgot my 'criticism' just now when I opened your book & read . . . 'I lifted impotent hands towards the stars.' It is a present which I may be able to thank you for some day.

I have had to give up my hope of going to Oxford. For in October I shall want £20; I have now 1/8½; and I foresee a period without work and without health.

Write to me when you can –

Yours ever
    Edward Thomas

<small>The quotation is from</small> The White Altar.

[13]

            Rose Acre
            6. vi. 02

My dear Jesse,

I sent copies of my book to Edwards and to my mother when I sent yours. Not one of them was acknowledged till today. I was worried & depressed & for the moment I was hurt. The peremptory postcard will very likely annoy Edwards, but I can't help it. As for you, my dear Jesse, don't think about it. Your letter was well worth the delay. I shall read it after each cruel review. You are most sympathetic, & I think all who really like the book will find it hard to criticise, because it has a personal warmth (I believe) in all its pages. What the unsympathetic reviewer will say I don't know; he has perhaps no right to say anything. The *Globe* reviewed me yesterday, & found me 'affected' & 'unsympathetic to the plain man', but was on the whole kind. Do you know that I myself am getting much pleasure out of the book? Only for a short time, I expect. You asked for two copies in your earlier letter. So I send them; if you don't want them, wait till I see you next; don't trouble to send them back.

'Echo' is a good word & a fine & I hope a true piece of criticism. I quite understand & wish I could be sure I deserved it. But I won't say anything more about Horae now, except to thank you for the *Pall Mall.*

Your letter was more to me than praise, & I know you meant it to be. Only just now such friendship as yours makes me feel the bitterness of my isolation more. It is that as well as my poverty I suffer from. If only you were near, I shouldn't mind sending to Sotheran my *Anatomy of Melancholy*, my *Arcadia*, my Beaumont & Fletcher, my Sir Thomas Browne & Fuller's *Worthies*, my *Walton's Lives* & in fact all I like, as I have been forced to do. But you will come again soon, won't you? Some friends want to come at the Coronation. Could you come then or before?

Today I am busy writing in great haste a paper on Holiday

Reading for *The Practical Teacher*, & I have mentioned *The White Altar* along with one or two other recent books – I hope you will not be hurt. I *made* the opportunity because I thought it might be useful.

I may go to Oxford this month or next. I wonder could you join me there for a day or two. Let me know.

Yes I know *Heu, miserande puer* in the 6th Aeneid. My 'Epitaph' is at once too serious & too trifling & perhaps out of harmony with the rest. If you can't come soon, I shall write again & perhaps visit you in town.

Yours ever with love to all

Edward Thomas

ET's new book was Horae Solitariae, *a collection of essays and prose sketches; 'Epitaphs as a Form of English Literature' was one of the few not reprinted in* Rose Acre Papers *in 1910. Edwards: Owen M. Edwards, to whom* Horae Solitariae *was dedicated; he had been ET's History tutor at Lincoln College. Sotheran: the London bookseller, who at this time had shops in the Strand and in Piccadilly. The Coronation of Edward VII was to take place on June 26, but was postponed until August 9 owing to the King's illness.*

[14]

Rose Acre
14. viii. 02.

My dear Jesse,

I am far too busy to write – busy contemplating my position and pretending to try to improve it. Here I sit like a fowl on an addled egg. It is fun to watch the favourable reviews – there have been many – coming one by one; & to see my essays coming back one by one. I find it hard sometimes to convince myself that after all the reviews are written by fools like myself & [therefore] don't count. But cider is a good drink & for 6d. I can make myself more sublime than Rothschild, Lord Kitchener or Guy Boothby. I have found an inn at the bottom of a hollow of the hills where I should like to sit for ever. I am off there now. When you come here – when will you come – you must join me there.

With best wishes to Mrs Berridge

Yours ever

Edward Thomas

Guy Boothby (1867-1905) was a prolific Australian novelist, who collected rare fish on his world travels, and bred prize dogs, horses and cattle.

Horsham. 14.viii.02.

My dear Jesse,

I am far too busy to write — busy contemplating my position and pretending to try to improve it. I feel sit like a fowl on an addled egg. It is fun to watch the favourable reviews — there have been many — coming in by one; & to see my essays coming back one by one. I find it hard sometimes to convince myself that after all the reviews are written by fools like myself, & I don't count. But cider is a good drink & for 6ᵈ. I can make myself more sublime than Rothschild, Lord Kitchener or Guy Boothby. I have found an inn at the bottom of a hollow of the hills where I should like to sit for ever. I am off there now. Therefore come here — when will you come — you must join me there. With best wishes to Mrs Berridge

Yours ever
Edward Thomas —

Facsimile of Edward Thomas's letter of 14 August 1902

[15]

Rose Acre
Bearsted
2. ix. 1902

My dear Jesse,

Your letter came just towards the end of a very blank month, & I really couldn't respond, except under the inspiration of cider, until now, when my luck seems to be improving. My only consolation was the housework I was bound to do. We were & we are without a servant & Helen can't do more than half the work. So I again widened my horizon by cleaning knives & scrubbing floors. I even began to have 'housemaid's knee', but that was a distinction I could not quite achieve. Now that I have a little work, it is hard to combine it with domesticities.

Everyone is away at the sea or among the mountains or in Italy, & I haven't seen anyone for a month or more. In any case I should have been disappointed at not seeing you – Please tell me how Mrs. Berridge is; & if you are too anxious for more, write a postcard at least. I hope she is comparatively well. . . . I often think of you at your Plato while I am at my Virgil or my beer, and I curse chance for separating these blisses which might so profitably be shared. When are you coming? Whenever you see a chance, let me know. If you don't come soon I may turn up some evening at Southfields. I look for news of the book. As for mine, the reviews are all favourable & often long. The last *Athenaeum* contains a very kind little notice. But the reviews don't help at all.

Helen & I send love to Mrs. Berridge and yourself.

Yours ever

Edward Thomas

JB had just moved to Elsenham Street, Southfields, a newly-built terrace in Wandsworth. His second book of sonnets was about to be published (see Letters 19 & 20). The 'very kind little notice' appeared, unsigned, in the Athenaeum of 30.8.02. To correct any impression that ET's prose work went unappreciated in his lifetime, it seems worth reprinting part of this very early and perceptive review here: "In Horae Solitariae, Mr Edward Thomas produces a very delicate example of old-fashioned essay-writing. He has no gospel to deliver or message to proclaim, but is content to walk in the ways of De Quincey and Charles Lamb, and has evidently come into the world to see, to meditate and to dream, rather than to do. A Celt of Wales, he stands a little aloof from the bustle of the dominant race, and loves sunrise and sunset, anglers, gardeners, the outline of trees against the sky, and the unrevealed secrets of unknown women's faces. . . . He can write, too, easily and with the fine distinction and without violence. . . . This is one of the books which keep alive in unfriendly days a tradition of scholarship and philosophic living to which we trust the world will return."

[16]

Rose Acre
16. ix. 1902

My dear Jesse,

I rejoice with you that everything is well. Let us have a bulletin now & then if you can't write more. The sight of your hand, even through the medium of not very elegant Latin, makes me wish for something more. You owe me a letter, too.

Have you time to get those books for me, second hand or new, preferably second-hand in duodecimo? –

I. Apuleius – (*Metamorph.*)
II. *Imitatio Christi.*
III. Boethius – *de Consolatione.*

I wouldn't bother you if there were a 2nd. hand shop within 30 miles. Another book I very much want is the Vulgate Bible. If you will buy any or all of these I will send payment. Neither of the 1st. three ought to cost more than 1/- do you think?

When are you coming here? Next month until about the 15th, (as well as this month) we are free. I should be very glad if you would come as soon as you are able.

Give my good wishes to Mrs. Berridge.

Yours ever
   P.E.T.

[17]

Rose Acre
24. ix. 1902

My dear Jesse,

I meant to see you on Monday but I had too much to do. Now I am back I can hardly answer your letter. For I am abed with a fever & quite disabled. I have thus put off the work which I have been planning during the rather empty 2 months just past. The whole time I wrote one or two reviews & made a page of notes. For I was housemaid here. I wish I had an engrossing study or rather, one more tangible than mine. Plotinus would be preferable. I now have Boethius & the Imitatio, not in translation wh could only spoil the sense. Think of the *Vision* of Boethius in English. Try to get a Vulgate, won't you?

My reviewers make me out a very fine chap, so I am forced to the extreme of humility. You should have seen the *Athenaeum*.

My best wishes to Mrs. Berridge & the baby (whose name is what?)

Yours ever
   Edward Thomas

JB's second son, Evan Denys, was born on 17 September.

[18]

Rose Acre
30. ix. 1902

My dear Jesse,

I am delighted to hear from you again. The Biblia is welcome, too; but if you should see one with larger print I should be glad of it. You ask me not 'to go the post office for' 1/-. So I shall try to remember to give you a book or two when you come next – I have several duplicates that you would like, e.g. Cawein's *Kentucky Poems*. You can always have any duplicate I possess, whether of review books or not. Remember that when you come.

Well, I soon got rid of my fever, but have not returned to my outdoor life. I have an exhausting cold. Still I have been doing a lot of work – reviews, and also an imaginary portrait. If you come down soon, you shall see it & much else that nobody will look at. We are half-engaged this weekend. But could you come? If so, let me know at once & I shall probably arrange it. Or would Saturday week be better?

I have done no new reading for months. The Aeneid, the Odyssey, the *Anatomy of Melancholy*, & Sir Philip Sidney are my home-field. Have you made any discovery?

Among my unfertilized plans still lies 'An essay on the Gospel of S. John, by a devout agnostic'. But I suppose no one would publish it.

Yes! isn't Belloc prodigious? But he is too unstable & fantastic to be anything more than a literary man. He ought to write more verses than he does.

I like Evan & Denys. I know many Evans in Wales. Do you know Treharne, Ivor, Meredith, & the rest, all Welsh like Evan? You cannot have a better name than Evan Denys. Commend me to him & to Mrs. Berridge. Heartily.

Ever yours
Edward Thomas

Cawein: Madison Julius Cawein (1865-1914), an American poet who published 36 volumes of verse; this selection was introduced by Edmund Gosse. On the day he wrote this letter, ET also began his long correspondence with Gordon Bottomley.

[19]

Rose Acre,
Bearsted
30. x. 1902

My dear Jesse,

Your letter comes at a busy moment. I am reviewing Leslie

Stephen who, though not a Platonist, is a fine writer: and item, a daughter arrived at 10.45 last night, leaving Helen out of breath but cheerful. Don't congratulate me; perhaps in 1920 you may. 'It' is an ugly, healthy thing, with a lot of black hair and blue eyes. Helen is very well today & sends her love to Mrs. Berridge. I am sorry she is not well, & only hope Evan Denys is. What shall we [call] it? There are no ugly names, I find. I incline to Mary, Rachel, Maudlin, – or Megalostrate! Perhaps it will be Rachel Mary, & if I have courage I shall insert Maudlin too, though 3 names are very unnecessary.

I shall look out for the sonnets. By the way I rather think I shall not review verse for the *Chronicle* again. I have got Gordon Bottomley's book. He sent it a fortnight ago & I have put it aside day after day. For I have been very busy & mainly with uncongenial books, & my poor little character sketch has been thrice rewritten & is as far from finished as ever. It is called 'A Saint' but may end as 'A Man'.

Try to write again soon. You see that I can't. I am quite well but, as you may suppose, lonelier than ever. Living all day alone makes me (physically) very tired. A three-mile walk tires me just as much as 30 miles with a friend. Still, I usually walk 12 miles a day. Tonight I dine with the Vicar, & I fear he will find me out as the godless philanderer I am. Up to day he appears to have thought me a Christian, but I can't be a Christian after wine.

Yours ever
Edward Thomas

ET reviewed Leslie Stephen's Studies of a Biographer, *volumes 3 & 4, in* DC *on 12.11.02. His second child was in fact named Rachel Mary Bronwen. Bottomley's book was* The Crier by Night, *a play. 'The Saint' eventually appeared in print as 'Philip Amberley,' one of the 'Dons Ancient & Modern' in* Oxford *(1903) – see Letter 24. There is an engaging description of the vicar and his wife in Helen Thomas's* World Without End, *ch. 4. The Revd. John Scarth was in the last year of his sixty years' incumbency. Jesse Berridge's sixty 'Sonnets of a Platonist' (1902) bore the epigraph: This flame of Spiritual Love / I set upon the Altar of Ideal Beauty.*

[20]

Rose Acre
7. xi. 1902

My dear Jesse,

I have been reading your sonnets carefully. I was struck at once by the advance you have made since *The White Altar*. The technique seems to me wonderfully good. There is barely a slip – except that you rhyme 'reveal' & 'ideal' & make these words into trisyllables. 'Some spiritual haven under quiet air'. I know the line can be defended, but it does not seem to me to be superior in music to a normal line. The word spirit has suffered much at the hands of Milton (who may have pronounced it 'sprite') and Tennyson; & I don't like to see it. Another improvement is – the way in which you have brought pauses in the sense almost invariably at the end of the line. You used to be inclined (like many another) to ignore the end of a line & let the sense swing on to the 2nd or 3rd syllable of a following line, with offence to harmony as well as sense. Here and there I find quite perfect lines like these – 'You breathe the roses of midsummer too, And winter's peace, & spring so much desired.' But I have made myself rather miserable by a feeling that I do not understand you sufficiently to see that there is a *sequence* of ideas or emotions in your series. And if I do not understand, you will hardly expect me to criticize. Yet I think I must say that you seem to me to have succumbed in places to the difficulties of dealing with an abstraction. In No. XXIII for example, you speak of a 'time-touched face', & I find it hard to believe that you do not mean a human face. Again, in No. XIV you say: 'Your verses found me in a happy hour. . .' Whose verses? (That sonnet by the way contains an ugly misprint – DANÆ.)

Personally, I have a dread of the sonnet. It must contain 14 lines, & a man must be a tremendous poet or a cold mathematician if he can accommodate his thoughts to such a condition. The result is – in my opinion – that many of the best sonnets are rhetoric only. I think most of Rossetti's are. Rossetti too is responsible for introducing the sesquipedalian-word sonnet, & he might have written the line
        'Philosophy's ideal incarnated'.
Sesquipedalian words are all very well & they are often magnificent – in you among others. But once under the spell, sense & concreteness are apt to disappear. That is so often in Rossetti. He expresses his emotion, if at all, by the sound of the words & not by their meaning. His sonnets are often like big men in pompous clothing. They are impressive without saying anything – and I really think you are inclined to follow him. I took you at your word. I took you as a 'Platonist' & I analysed & paraphrased several sonnets – and I think I found too little substance. I fear you will quarrel with the method. But then all of Shakespeare's will bear it. I don't mean that every sonnet should contain a fresh & striking idea that would look well in a leading article. I mean that if a sonnet fails to produce an impression of strength & unity, & if, on analysis, it still seems to lack unity & strength, then it is inconsiderable.

Frankly, I think you are not quite justified in calling yourself a Platonist. That you have read and loved him there is no doubt. But that you have read all of him & thoroughly digested his work after a comparison with philosophers of other schools, I am inclined to disbelieve. For Plato's *ideas* seem to me as concrete as Goethe's *men & women* – You on the other hand conspicuously lack concreteness; you seem to realize it yourself, & to make up for it by a blend of the real & the ideal. N.B. I use 'concrete' figuratively, to imply clearness & firmness. A Platonist, it seems to me, is one who, having mastered Plato, builds upon the foundations laid by Plato. That is, he is not a disciple so much as a successor. You, on the other hand, seem to have been content to do as I should do myself, i.e. to take a hint from a phrase or passage in Plato, and to let it germinate in your own brain. That is not Platonism! It is the higher plagiarism, & I know something about that.

Frankly, in the second place, I don't think the sonnet suits you – you have written sonnets that are lovely in form. But I think it encourages your aerial tendency too much. It compels you to use words loosely, to forget that words have a value beyond their sound. Thus, I think that, as far as feeling & substance go, some of your lyrics are far superior to your sonnets, simply because you have the lyrical impulse (your sonnets show it) & because you have more freedom in variable measures.

In conclusion, nothing will please me better than a proof that (1) you are a Platonist & (2) you are a born sonneteer.

Yours ever
    Edward Thomas

[21]

Rose Acre
19. xi. 1902

My dear Jesse,

Your letter helps me a good deal. The worst I said of your Sequence was the result of a contradiction between the purport of your sonnets & what you said of them when I saw you last. Perhaps you weren't clear then; probably I was obtuse. Anyhow, your explanation now makes the matter almost plain. If I review the book, I will keep your letter by me. But I hope I didn't omit to say that I thought (and my experience is, of necessity, wide) that your technical excellence was remarkable & pretty well unique, among very moderns. Still, lyrics, more lyrics, please!

I hope I shall see you very soon. I was in town last week-end, but couldn't get over to Southfields. Now I have a small job which will take me to the British Museum for at least two days. I am editing *John Dyer*, you know, & the printer waits for copy. By the way, should you see a copy of Dyer (e.g. the 1765 edition) going for 3 or 4 shillings let me know at once. I have only one, & of course the printer wants one.

I am otherwise busy too, and I haven't a moment for any hobby horse. – My daughter will probably bear the burden of these three names – Rachel Mary Bronwen.

Please remember Helen & me to your wife. Our love to you.

Yours ever
Edward Thomas

P.S. I shall very likely be in town on Friday & Saturday. Will you let me know what day I may call?

[22]

[*address missing*]
3. xii. 1902

My dear Jesse,

Thank you very much. Shall I mention you in my preface? But you have saved me 5/- and time, I hope without any big waste on your own part. 'Aurelia' struck me as being pretty in its 18th century way & quite good enough for Dyer. Oh the dull boot-black labour he has given me. Yet he was a good man.

I sent you 2/- because I owed you 2/-. I would have sent the other 1/- before but it didn't seem worth while. You shall still have the books I spoke of, though I find I have only one copy of Cawein (I have to return my *World* review books).

My latest book is Churton Collins's *In Memoriam &c*. He 'edits' it, i.e. he shows how much can be said about it by a foolish well-read man.

I have another book in hand. It is called *House Mottoes & Inscriptions* & is by a real lunatic. Now I know nothing of lunacy & only from that point of view is the. . . [*half a line missing*] . . . But I know very little. . . [*half a line missing*] . . . want to write an essay. . . [*half a line missing*] . . . wonder do you know any. If you do, send them to me, as you love me. Mottoes over gates, round friezes, on lintels, or in pubs are what I want, but not

Customers came and I did trust 'em
I lost their money & their custom.

If you can imagine any, equally good, *what would you put* round your wall, or on your mantelpiece, or on your hearth, or over your door? ' "Continuance maketh Hell" – and Heaven'? I saw a pretty one on a clock the other day – '*Le moment où je parle est déjà loin de nous.*' And over a disembowelled clock at a pub – 'No tick,' and over a Jew grocer's – 'To patronise us pleases you and us,' and round a beautiful Thames-beholding room 'Sweete Themmes runne softly till I ende my song.'

Yes, I think we shall be free on Saturday week. So I hope to see you then.

Love from us to you both,

Ever yours
  Edward Thomas

<small>John Churton Collins was an academic writer on English literature and a notoriously severe critic; ET was reviewing his edition of Tennyson's longer poems. The 'lunatic' author was S. F. A. Caulfield, (reviewed in DC 8.1.03).</small>

[23]

Rose Acre
[9]. xii. 1902

My dear Jesse,

I shall expect you on Saturday, by the train you took before, leaving Holborn about 2.35 (or Victoria, which you like), & reaching Bearsted at 4.30. Of course I will meet you there.

I hope you weren't hurt at all by my review, (assuming that you care what reviewers say,) and I apologize for the printer's error – but I had no proofs.

I like '*Noctem quietam et finem perfectam concedat Deus omnipotens.*' But I am still unable to write my paper on house-mottoes.

Saturday then.

Yours ever
  Edward Thomas

<small>The Latin is from the Office of Compline: 'The Lord Almighty grant us a quiet night and a perfect end.' ET reviewed **The Sonnets of a Platonist** in the DC on 5.12.02, with nine other new volumes of verse (including Bottomley's verse play **The Crier by Night**). He writes: "Mr Berridge sets '*this flame of spiritual love upon the Altar of Ideal Beauty.*' His sonnet sequence is, in the first place, the narrative of an imaginary Platonist's love for a friend who embodies his 'ideal,' to use a vague word appropriate to the vague notions of this book. The narrative is diversified by incidents – absence, the sending of verses from one to another, and letters of encouragement and praise. In the second place, it is the study of a soul that is uplifted by the love of beauty, spiritual and physical. The sequence is by no means an obvious one. But the sixty sonnets make a complete whole of exaltation, beauty, sentiment, and mist. We confess ourselves somewhat out of sympathy with these empyreal doings. At the same time, we</small>

think that the book is one that withholds its choicest savours from the unsympathetic. That is to say, that it is not so lucid in thought and definite in expression as it ought to be; but also, that it will (like so much verse not of the first rank) have a high value for its best lovers."

[24]

Rose Acre,
Bearsted,
nr Maidstone
1. i. 1903

My dear Jesse,

Yes, I have been busy, & I know I ought to have writ before. Yesterday & today I have been preparing a long obituary of —— who is at the point of death, I believe. And I had to do the new "Milton" – *Nova Solyma* – at intervals I have done some strokes of original work – 'On lighting the first fire in Autumn'. The 'Saint' turned out not quite a Saint as I wrote. So I called the paper 'Philip Amberley: a silhouette of an old man.' You shall see it when you come.

I am so glad everyone praises your sonnets. I quite feel they deserve it: only I am not the right, predestined reader for them. You have never shown me your Faun. I look forward to it; for I have not seen your drawing at all.

Horae is getting on quietly, with good reviews now & then, especially in the New York *Nation*.

How kind of your son to think me worthy to write for children; & I hope he does like the book. When are you coming down?

Good wishes to you all –
Ever yours
Edward Thomas

ET does not name the subject of the obituary. Nova Solyma *was an anonymous Latin romance, first published in 1648. Its translator, Rev. Walter Begley, ascribed it to Milton, and ET in his* DC *review (18.12.02) says: 'It is certainly either the work of Milton or of some inconceivably industrious and brilliant intimate of his.' The Faun: one of many pen and ink drawings done by JB in the earlier part of his life, many of them in the Beardsley manner then fashionable.*

[25]

13 Rusham Road,
Nightingale Lane, S.W.
12. ii. 1903

My dear Jesse,

I have come alone to live in town for an indefinite length of time, because I am in debt, & am not earning much nor likely to, for some months. Could you meet me *outside* the Pharos Club at 5.45 tomorrow (Friday)? Anyhow, I will be there. I shall probably not have anything to do in the evening, but don't want to go to Southfields because of the railway fare. I have only a few shillings until I get work. So if you know any journalist, or any likely persons, please introduce me.

Ever yours
   Edward Thomas

The Balham address was that of ET's parents from 1902 until Mr Thomas's death in 1920. The house has since been re-numbered as 12.

[26]

Rose Acre,
Bearsted
14. vi. 1903

My dear Jesse,

Why haven't you come down before this? On Wednesday, the 17th., we move to Bearsted Green, & I hope you will come very soon. Please let me know whether you can come down on the 20th. or 27th. I expect my mother on one of those days, so if you can keep both open & allow me to decide which, I should be very glad. The book is practically finished, i.e. I have still to copy out a chapter on the Oxford country. I have already sent in the following

 1 On entering Oxford
 2 The Stones of Oxford
 3 Dons Ancient and Modern
 4 Undergraduates of the Present & the Past
 5 College Servants " " " " "
 6 An Oxford Day
 7 Old Oxford Days
 8 From a College Garden
10 In Praise of Oxford

Most of it is either dull or drivelling.

Please remember us all to Mrs. Berridge

Yours ever
   Edward Thomas

[27]

Bearsted Green
22. xii. 03

My dear Jesse,

I am home again for a short time – just home – & soon I expect to go to Tintagel or to sea. And I am so glad to hear from you again. Nowadays I never can write letters & I never receive them in consequence.

Still, here are some facts. Warminster did me good tho I had to work as usual. I take codliver oil, cocoa, much beef & milk, no tea, no narcotics, & little exercise. For I have to avoid exhaustion. But how far my brain will be restored I can't say. Sincerely, I am not hopeful, tho I am glad to say that I brood rather less. You have heard of the *Chronicle* changes – a new Scotch editor, a new Scotch literary editor, & reduced expenses (it is rumoured). I expect to suffer heavily, & must try the 'Daily News' & perhaps the new papers. – Yes, of course, I want something regular, e.g. a librarianship.

Oxford is out, & full of printer's errors in spite of my corrections – 'morn' for 'moon' – '19th' for '13th' century &c. It can't help me, & even if it were very well received I am powerless to take advantage of it. For I can't write even a short review without an effort before & exhaustion and dissatisfaction after. An essay is inconceivable.

Who is printing your collection of Sonnets? – You are too busy, I am sure, unless (which I doubt) your office work is soothing.

Here is a guinea. The loan is so old that I have no doubt the payment will surprise you. Don't talk about my not repaying it, or I shall never be able to borrow of you again!

Helen & I send our love to you all.

Yours ever
Edward Thomas

'To sea'; *ET was considering sailing to Canada to join his St Paul's and Oxford friend, Ian MacAlister (1878-1957), who was ADC to the General commanding the Canadian Army from 1902 to 1904. The editorship of the* Daily Chronicle, *at 80 Fleet Street, was about to pass from W. J. Fisher (who had succeeded H. W. Massingham in 1899) to Robert Donald (to 1918). More importantly for ET, his friend H. W. Nevinson, literary editor since 1899 (and dedicatee of* The Heart of England *in 1906) was to be succeeded by James Milne, whom ET could neither like nor respect. However, his reviews continued to appear regularly in the* DC *until 1911, and occasionally thereafter until 1914.*

[28]

Elses Farm
The Weald
Sevenoaks
21. vii. 04

My dear Jesse,
I am very glad to hear from you again. We moved two months

Edward Thomas about 1904

ago. Since then I have only been once in town or I should have looked you up. I only wish you could come over here this weekend. But you can't leave Edna, can you? Give her my best wishes, & say that if she would like to spend a week here with the new baby we should like it and especially Helen. A week as soon as she is well enough to stand a 3 mile drive from the station hither. Don't forget.

Very likely I shall have a day in town next Wednesday. If I call at the Bank at 5 what could you do?

I wish I could help you even with advice in the matter of money. A novel need not be paying, of course. But if you are equal to writing anything fairly light & easily read, I am sure the *Week's Survey* would like it. Send things often but not over 1000 words & if possible 800. If you could collect a volume of essays, I know a publisher who would probably take them & give you a *small royalty*. Call at the *Daily Chronicle*, try to get theological books or ecclesiastical history.

If I were more successful I could help you more. But I am very badly off at this moment, with 5/- in hand and a prospect of only £1 this month & debts accumulating!

'The Skeleton' came to an end only a week or two ago. That and a very little complaint about the destruction of an old house near Clapham Junction are all, except reviews, that I have written this year. And I am still dejected and relaxed tho we like this house very much. Helen & the children are very well.

Do you see Frank Dyall & Dal now that they are neighbours?

Ever yours with our love to you all

Edward Thomas

Elses Farm was the Thomases' home from May 1904 until December 1906; Helen Thomas later looked back on this as the happiest period of her life. The new baby was Christian Gerard Berridge, born on July 3rd. 'The Skeleton' was an essay portraying a beautiful youth in spring and his skeleton in autumn; it was published in 1905 in The Venture *No. 2 (ed. John Baillie) (see ET's* Letters to Gordon Bottomley, *ed. R. G. Thomas, nos. 12 & 15). Frank Dyall (1870-1950) was an actor, Charles Dalmon (1872-1938) a poet. (see Introduction, p. 12).*

[29]

Elses Farm,
The Weald
16. ix. 04.

My dear Jesse,

I am glad to hear you had a good holiday & I should like to have shared part of it with you here or at Oxford. But it was impossible.

How silly of you to talk about offending me. You never will. And on this occasion I should have been offensive indeed if I had been offended. I understand perfectly. No doubt you are busy and poor. I only envy you your will. I ought to be both busy and careful. But I have no anchor or ballast, & I waste time & money on even unpleasant & inessential things. But don't accuse me of supposing that you are the same or ought to be. Come when you can, and if you feel penitential write me another letter and don't mention it.

I should like to walk into Oxford from Tiddington with you some day.

I haven't fished much, for I have no heart to fish or walk alone.

I have the usual dull books to review. I do the usual dull reviews and worse. Nothing else. I am sick of books and am selling many old possessions now (prose; never poetry, I hope). Ruskin is the first to go. I want to begin again & this is my frantic and vain protest.

You are to be conspicuous in the *Week's Survey* this week. The prose is excellent. I am very glad.

Remember me to your wife and to Dell. Will you bring him over, some day?

Goodbye, with our love –

Yours ever

Edward Thomas

The Week's Survey of Politics, Literature and Commerce. *price one penny, lasted from 1901 to 1906. The issue of 17.9.04 reprinted JB's sonnet 'After Death' from* The White Altar, *and also carried a short prose piece by JB entitled 'Compline.' ET himself was a frequent contributor to the paper at this time.*

[30]

The Weald
22. xii. 04.

My dear Jesse,

We all come to town for Christmas tomorrow, & I want to see you. I wonder will you be at all free on Friday night or Christmas Eve? If I don't appear tomorrow, would you send a word to

13 Rusham Road,
Balham S.W.

saying whether you are free on Saturday at all?

I have done many things – all foolish – since I saw you last : –

I expected to see you at Chelsea

I agreed to write a book on Wales for Blacks.

I left Chelsea & went to Wales & had some immortal days.

Then I came here to work & have had nothing but complete misery & a week in bed & work all day.

The book is half done: for as usual it has to be done in haste: & is infinitely worse than Oxford.

If these fables seem not too abstract for your heir, give the book to him with a heathen's blessing.

With good wishes from Helen & me to you & Edna & all.

Ever yours
Edward Thomas

ET *took a room at 1 Gunter Grove, Chelsea, for a few weeks in September and October 1904. His friend Arthur Ransome (1884-1967) had taken another room in the house (see his* Autobiography, *ed. R. Hart-Davis, 1976, p. 99). Ransome's recollection in old age of his and ET's first visit to Duncan Williams's flat in Gray's Inn Road in 1903 is surely inaccurate, since ET had met Williams and been to his flat at least two years earlier. In November ET and Helen visited his Welsh cousins at Ammanford in Carmarthenshire, and ET went walking alone in the mountains of Cardiganshire for four days. What fables ET presented to Dell is not known.*

[31]

The Weald,
Sevenoaks
16. iv. 05.

My dear Jesse,

The cuckoo came last Monday, the nightingale on Friday: when are you coming? Can it be the first week end in May – the 6th? If not, do choose an early one, & we will fish. I haven't seen you this year, have I? And you haven't written. So I shall take it hard if you do not come. "Wales" is done & nearly forgotten: if you have time to read it I will send you a perfect proof. Nothing has happened that will go on paper today, but we are all well. I hope you all are.

Ransome has another book out – a gallant, sweet, unnoticeable thing. He prospers & comes here sometimes.

By the way, I now work in a little cottage, $\frac{1}{2}$ a mile over the fields from here. An Oxford friend of mine – whom you will perhaps like – has rented it & comes for weekends or so.

Goodbye. I salute you & all yours: so does Helen & so do Merfyn & the merry one (she often remembers Jesse).

Ever yours
Edward Thomas

Ransome's book was The Stone Lady: ten little papers and two mad stories. *The Oxford friend was Martin Freeman (see note to Letter 33). The cottage in Egg-Pie Lane, occupied by W. H. Davies at ET's invitation for several months from February 1906, has since disappeared.*

[32]

The Weald
25. vii. 05.

My dear Jesse,

Only a word. I have not read Inge's *Christian Mysticism*. Perhaps you were going to send it me. Don't be angry if I say, please do not send it. I shouldn't be able to read it. I can't read anything but review books. I am in a horrible state. You are too kind and hopeful to believe me if I try to explain, & I know you are misled by my jesting, my apparent good health, & the many things that ought to make me happy (as you think). But write whenever you can.

If I come to town next week, I can't meet Chesterton.

Yours with Helen's love
Edward Thomas

[33]

The Weald
8. viii. 05.

My dear Jesse,

I did call at the Bank last Wednesday at 10 minutes to 5 & was sorry to find you gone. I half expected to see you at the Vegetarian Restaurant between 5 & 6: I am almost always there on every other Wednesday. But I fear you were still unwell – I hope you are right now. Perhaps I shall feel more equal to meeting Chesterton later: if I do, I shall want you to take me.

I am glad to have your letter tho I do not know what is the 'one cure' for me. I can only think about 'cures' when I am fairly well & then I can't think very seriously. The one thought which may in the end be comforting is that there is certainly no hope from myself or the tenderest friend.

Of course I know books & reviews are not important, but vanity prevents me from treating them quite lightly as well as badly.

What I really ought to do is to live alone. But I can't find courage to do the many things necessary for taking that step. It is really the kind H & the dear children who make life almost *impossible*.

Freeman & I started for Canterbury on Saturday but we only did 25 miles because my foot became blistered. We had one good night sleeping under corn sheaves in a field not far from where you & I slept one day – on the Pilgrim's Road. I meant to have asked you to come & strangely forgot.

Yours ever
Edward Thomas

<small>The St George's (Vegetarian) Restaurant was at 37 St Martin's Lane, next to the Coliseum. A. Martin Freeman (1878-1960) was at Lincoln College with ET. He became an authority on Irish literature and Gaelic folksongs; ET's Feminine Influence on the Poets is dedicated to him.</small>

[34]

The Weald
16. x. 05.

My dear Jesse,

You really ought to write to me. You know what I am doing perfectly well – grumbling & wearing my clothes & doing reviews for the million. But I don't know in the least why you are in East Ham. Have you been kidnapped? If so, what is your ransom? I might subscribe. If you have not been kidnapped, why are you there? Perhaps you don't like writing any more than I do. Then I wish you could meet me in town. You are up sometimes, I expect. I shall probably be up – if two lame feet allow me – next Wednesday week. Where can I meet you?

I met a poet the other day.

William H. Davies
Farmhouse (lodging house)
Marshalsea Road, S.E.

His book is *The Soul's Destroyer* which is full of things that nobody else could have written in 20 years. Try to see them or him.

With Helen's love & mine to you all.

Edward Thomas

<small>JB was living for a few months in Rancliffe Road, East Ham, preparing for ordination; his youngest son, Wilfrid Hugh, was born there on 6.6.06 (see Letter 35). W. H. Davies (1871-1940): ET's review of his first book of poems (DC 21.10.05) – under the heading A POET AT LAST! – helped Davies immensely: 'I have often wondered idly how I should meet the apparition of a new poet – it was so easy to praise small or middling writers of verse – and now all I can do is to help lay down a cloak of journalists' words, over which he may walk a little more easily to his just fame. . . . His greatness rests upon a wide humanity, a fresh and unbiased observation, and a noble use of the English tongue.'</small>

[35]

*The Weald,
nr Sevenoaks*
23. v. 06.

My dear Jesse,

Allright. I am sorry I missed you. When your examination is

over – when is it? – let me know & come down for the inside of a week or Friday to Monday. I have no engagements now, but shall be busy for a few weeks because I have still to copy out the chapters of a book I have written during the last two months. We leave here at Michaelmas or before & probably go to Petersfield near Selborne, in Hampshire, to be near a very good school for Merfyn: tomorrow I go to look at a house there, & if I can get back in time I will call at St. George's between 5 & 6. We are all well, especially the children. I hope Edna is better now. You must get a country curacy, & take her away from London.

With our love to you all
Ever yours
    Edward Thomas

ET and his family moved to Berryfield Cottage at Ashford, near Steep, early in December, so that Mervyn could attend Bedales School nearby.

[36]
Berryfield Cottage,
Ashford,
Petersfield
1. i. 07.

My dear Jesse,

Smoking some of your York River tobacco, but otherwise rather denuded by too long a walk into Sussex in the slush, I thank you for your letter and the tobacco. I am glad you liked the books. If I could possibly help to set Dell off in a direction of profit & delight I should be happy. I wish I had got to know him. But now he is getting older & aloof I expect, how hard it is to get over the natural boundaries between those even of an age I know, I know; for here I am surrounded by good men, masters at Bedales school, & so far I simply look at them with a 'how I wonder what you are.' How I wish you were a curate – or better still a rector – within an easy walk. Someday you & I ought to walk to Oxford from here. Winchester is a fine day's walk, Selborne is close at hand.

Never mind now about the tunes. I sang them to Freeman & now we have got them all right. You shall have the Anthology & recommend it to your parishioners as by your brother. The melodies – 56 of them – are a fine lot but the poems are perhaps rather obviously chosen by one who didn't want to clash with other anthologists.

Some day I will come to Colchester. Tell me when it is quite convenient & I will do my best.

Davies is cheerful at the cottage & looking out for reviews of his *New Poems* just published by Elkin Mathews. Ransome is at present in Edinburgh where his mother lives. He is or lately was engaged again & he has plenty of work – did $\frac{1}{2}$ a dozen Xmas books for children, of no great merit. Tom is in Derbyshire, cheerful & serene & puzzling as ever I suppose. Rolf has a boy baby. Yes I saw Hogg's book & gave it a lift in the *D.C.* Some of it was jolly good, clear & original thoughts justly expressed. But I never got the *Virgin Goddess.* I wish I had. Lend it to me some day.

Merfyn had 10 days at school at the end of a term & now looks forward to his scarlet cap & school every day with joy. He was a Rat in a musical performance of the Pied Piper of Hamelin at the end of the term.

Helen's love & mine to you and Edna and Dell & Denys and *incogniti* Tertius & Quartus.

Yours ever
   Edward Thomas

> *The Anthology is* The Pocket Book of Poems and Songs for the Open Air, *compiled by ET and published in 1907; the Revd. Jesse Berridge, now a curate at St. Botolph's, Colchester, is thanked in the Introduction for 'the three new sea songs.' Tom Clayton was a school friend of ET's; Rolf was probably a publisher's reader. Hogg's book: Walter Hogg's* Meditata, *a collection of fifty sonnets, was reviewed by ET on 17.11.06, when he refers to the sonnet as 'a form which has many temptations to declamation, redundance, and obscurity,' but adds that 'as a rule [Mr Hogg] succeeds in expressing a serious and passionate thought with such grace that we are not offended, as we usually are in reading sonnets, by any grandiosity in the form.'* The Virgin Goddess: *a poetical tragedy by Rudolf Besier, produced at the Adelphi Theatre in 1906 and published in 1907; the author gave JB an inscribed copy. 'Incogniti Tertius and Quartus' were JB's third and fourth sons, Christian and Wilfrid, whose names were as yet unknown to ET.*

[37]

       Berryfield Cottage,
       Ashford,
       Petersfield
       20. iii. 07.

My dear Jesse,

I am sorry for your news. I had no suspicion of it & that makes me angry with myself. But I did wonder why you never wrote & we never met in town. Soon we must. There is no news from us. At this moment I am at Devizes in Wiltshire & am walking about for 3 days on the Downs & in Savernake forest; I came on here on Monday from Chepstow where I had 4 days: altogether a week's holiday taken unexpectedly & with such enjoyment as I can manage. I wonder where you saw a nice review of *Heart of England*? No I have no new books in hand, & only vaguely dream of one on the fleeting old things – old homes & bits of green &c – in the suburbs – of course a very little book. *The Book of the Open Air* is just coming out, I think, & the Anthology will be out next month. But this is no time for a real letter because I am about to start on a last walk here, & tomorrow I shall begin to be very busy at home – only reviewing.

We should all send our love to you all, if we were together. Mine now to all of you.

Ever yours
    Edward Thomas

JB had been with his mother when she died of cancer at Tiddington on 11 February, at the age of 60.

[38]
    Northampton
    [*undated*: early June 1907]

My dear Jesse,

Just a word to salute you & say we are all well. I have stayed here a night on my way to Bottomley at Cartmel near Windermere. There I am to walk & to read the fiction of Richard Jefferies, because my next book is most likely to be a life of him. Messrs. Hutchinson have asked me to do it. A year's work & not much pay. But it will be worth while. Don't mention it to anyone lest it should get round to some smart and willing youth who will do it for Harmsworth in a fortnight or 3 weeks. I put your letter in my bag but that is at the station & I must write now or not for a long while. I am very glad you liked the Pocket Book. It has some nice things in it & you will like the songs especially

    Greensleeves
    Men of Gotham
    When thou must home
    Wraggle Taggle Gipsies

Let me tell you of some misprints.
In Amarillys – '*sien*' should be '*rien*' – '*ou*' should be '*or*'
In '*la fille du Roi*', '*mère*' should be '*mène*'.
In *Meum est propositum* '*ceterni*' should be '*aeterni*'
        '*upsam*'   '*ipsam*'
        '*negne*'   '*neque*'
        '*ebrus*'   '*ebriis*'

in Keats' 'Psyche'	'rose' should be 'rosy'
in 'Dowsabell'	'half undight' 'hall undight'.
in Keats' 'Fancy'	'joy' (near end) should be 'joys'
in Browning's 'Last Ride' 'brain's	'brains'

in 'Poor old Horse' one line should be 'hang him, whip him, stick &c'
& another 'over hedges, bridges, brooks *and* bridges.'

Will you come down this Summer? If not I shall certainly come to see you. It is no good my writing letters now. I *have* to write so many that I dislike that I can't enjoy any.

News. Frank & Dal are living at Hampton-on-Thames & Frank (I hear) is engaged to the lovely Phyllis Logan. But I haven't seen them this year. Duncan is marrying again – Margaret MacGregor.

Now I have to go out. Goodbye. My love to you all.

Ever yours
Edward Thomas

<small>Gordon Bottomley (1874-1948), poet and dramatist, lived at this time at Well Knowe, an isolated farmhouse near Cartmel. Duncan Williams married his second wife on 29 June. (His divorced first wife had married Jacob Epstein the previous year). The only child of the second marriage, Alan Meredith, eventually became British ambassador in Madrid.</small>

[39]

Berryfield Cottage,
Ashford,
Petersfield
21. vi. 07.

My dear Jesse,

Your letter reached me at Cartmel near Windermere where I was having a fortnight with Bottomley in the rain. I was walking or talking all day & had to work hard all evening. I got back here yesterday & found the roses out & the hay harvest well begun & everyone well. Now I have to work at the Jefferies. Helen & I will probably take our short holiday at Coate where he was born & lived 30 years, though I have already known it 20 years myself. but only for 2 or 3 days, I fear. About July 29?

Helen & I are very glad to say that what we know of Bedales through our own visits & through the reports of parents & masters & through meeting some of the children, boys & girls, is entirely in its favour. We have had no disappointment, & you know we had formed great hopes of it. Helen has taught at the Preparatory School there for 2 terms now – an hour or so a day. Probably the little Noel would go to the Preparatory & that we know really well. The headmaster R. Scott & his wife are admirable. That is where Mervyn is: the children there number about 30 & are between the ages of 7 & 12 or so.

I haven't heard from Frank or Dal about the engagement yet.

Until we meet then. Goodbye & love to you all.

Ever yours
    Edward Thomas

'The little Noel' was the youngest daughter of Sir Sydney Olivier. It was through her that ET met Rupert Brooke, who fell in love with her while she was at Bedales; ET and his wife helped the two to meet without the Olivier family's knowledge (see Jan Marsh: Edward Thomas, *pp. 104-5).*

[40]

Berryfield Cottage,
Ashford,
Petersfield
20. x. 07.

My dear Jesse,

It is a month since your note came and yet I am no better able to write a letter back than I was then. It is so easy to fill all my time with necessary reading, writing & gardening that I never even have a walk nowadays except just to get warm & a little less muddled in the mornings. Of course I could always find *time* to write to you. But a mere half hour wedged in among work doesn't make a letter & if I sit down to write one I think of a hundred irrelevant things. The little time I can spare seems to go more & more to London where I can be sure of having a good talk at any rate. At the beginning of November I am going to have a fortnight in town, I expect, as I must read in the Museum for almost a fortnight before I can start on Jefferies. Now that there are so many new books & reviewing abounds it is hard to get time for the biography. But I spent yesterday on copying the important parts of 60 of his youthful letters to an Aunt & Uncle. I have still many books bearing on Jefferies to read & some of his own to reread & analyse. How it rains! Yet I just look up and then ignore it. I should like to walk 20 miles in it – with you, Jesse. How are you all? We are well enough & the children very well. Is it possible you will be in town in the first half of November? If so let me know in time to arrange a meeting. Write when you can. Our love to you all.

Yours ever
    Edward Thomas

[41]

Berryfield Cottage,
Ashford,
Petersfield
1. xi. 07.

My dear Jesse,

Many thanks for Behmen. Do any of your books go into the question of the origin of mysticism, I mean psychologically, showing what all mystics have in common, & discussing the meaning of 'vision', 'inspiration' & so on? I want to get at what Jefferies, a non-Christian mystic in one of his books, has in common with the others, & as I only know a few others I should like some help from outside, if possible. It is possible I shall see you soon as I may go to a cottage near Dunwich (to write my book) some time within a month & perhaps Colchester is on my way or could be made to seem so.

Goodbye with my love to you all,
Yours ever
Edward Thomas

Jacob Behmen or Boehme (1575-1624): a German shoemaker whose mystical speculations influenced William Blake.

[42]

125 Anerley Road,
Anerley S.E.
Saturday
[9. 11. 07.]

My dear Jesse,

Your letter has only just found me here & the books must wait till I get back. I wish I had been able to write back at once. The books sound as if they will be useful and after your dear letter I am sure I shall be as fit as I ever can be to receive what they have to give. I too wish we were together now. But you should not talk about my being 'indulgent'. Of course I am not.

I have just finished my first week at the British Museum, a tedious week & not very fruitful. Probably I go home on Friday next. Then I have to spend a few days in Wiltshire & then about December 5 I shall probably go to Suffolk. Let me know if I shall see you on my way.

With my love to you all
Yours ever
Edward Thomas

The South London address was that of Harry and Janet Hooton. Janet was one of Helen Thomas's oldest friends and a witness at her wedding (her maiden name was Aldis – see Letter 44). Harry became one of ET's intimate friends; The Icknield Way *was dedicated to him.*

[43]

21. xii. 07.

My dear Jesse,

Here is a book for Dell, & one for you & my love to you all. And here are your books back again. I ruined my chances of getting any real good from them by approaching them in my now almost perpetual fume & hurry. It was impossible to read them all so I had to leave *Immanence* untouched & read only a quarter of Inge & I got something to the purpose – to the immediate purpose – out of Inge, but my own soul remains a blasted heath: Perhaps when I come to look at Jefferies more intently I shall be the better for it. Well, I leave home on Friday next & on the 28th go to Minsmere, nr Dunwich in Suffolk for 2 months or so to write the Jefferies, or to make a first draft. You didn't say whether Colchester was likely to be on the way or not, so I suppose it wasn't. I don't yet know what my station is. All I know is I am to leave Liverpool Street at 11.45 a.m. on Saturday the 28th. Perhaps you can see from the timetable whether that is a train that stops at Colchester. If so, then I might come by an earlier one & have an hour with you. Let me know (if you are able) whether this is possible. If not I will see you on my way back. We are all well & have had no illnesses at all. I have been much in town to the Museum &c & once again to Wiltshire. All my material is ready now, all I am likely to get, & I tremble to be at it in quiet & solitude. Goodbye. Wish me luck.

I am ever yours
    Edward Thomas

The address has been torn off this letter, which is written on ET's 'Berryfield' notepaper.

[44]

*Minsmere,
nr Dunwich,
Saxmundham,
Suffolk*
10. i. 08.

My dear Jesse,

I am glad you liked the books, & sorry I didn't see you on my way here: I looked out at Colchester in vain. Well, I may be passing through on Friday the 24th. Might I be able to see you then? I have to go to see a doctor in town. I have at last laid myself at the feet of a specialist who has commanded many abstentions and given me medicines which seem to make me very comfortable but to lessen my working power. He won't say yet what is the matter with me. However, I have begun Jefferies & in fact made quite a hole in the work this week. The Aldises live in the next cottage & Maud who was staying here asked much after you. She seems a very good woman indeed & she plays the viola gloriously. Well, I am very busy & have to get my walk now. So goodbye with love to you all.

Ever yours
Edward Thomas

Did you hear Frank Dyall married Phyllis Logan?

Frank Dyall's bride was one of the 'three lovely daughters' of Helen's friend Beatrice Logan (later Mrs Potbury) of Hammersmith (see note to Letter 28). They were married at Kingston in autumn 1907 and their son Valentine was born the following year.

[45]

Minsmere,
nr Dunwhich,
Suffolk
17. ii. 08.

My dear Jesse,

I believe I can get to you & back for a few shillings. Could you put me up for one night? It would have to be Saturday, though, as that is the only day of cheap tickets. And then I see I could not leave Colchester till 5.30 & you would be busy all of Sunday. Next Saturday I mean.

Or I could break my journey on March 3 for a few hours or, if convenient to you, for the night. Tell me which to do.

I have gone on steadily with Jefferies writing a lot of dull stuff I am sure, what else I don't know. I get tired of this flat country & now that one of the children here has gone I find them poorish company & would prefer solitude.

How are you? and Edna & the children? It seems so feeble not to be able to get over to you when I am so near. Helen is well but the children have been having measles and Bronwen is still in the rash stage but feeding on chocolate & lemonade by a doctor's advice her life must be worth living.

This is only a note between sleeping & waking at midnight, but with my love to you all.

Ever yours
Edward Thomas

Did you know Frank Dyall married Phyllis Logan months ago?

[46]

Minsmere
26. ii. 08.

My dear Jesse,

I am a muddler. I see that unless I leave Dereham at 7.18 I can't reach Colchester until 2.15. so that if you have theatricals in the afternoon that is no good, & the 7.18 is impossible as we are 6½ miles from the station. What can be done? Helen comes here for the weekend to recover from nursing the children (the latest diet for measles is chocolate & lemonade) & would have liked to see you all. But it really does look impossible. I am sorry I did not look up ways and means before. In any case if it can't be managed, we can meet before very long. You know that if you can ever get away you will be welcome at home, & if you can't then I shall come to Colchester. I am in a greater hurry than ever now. Hooton came for the weekend: I have a good but difficult book of poems to review; I have *Jefferies* to finish – the first draft – before Friday. What a pity you aren't a letter writer, for then I could get some satisfaction by writing back, but it is only a long letter that can get a long letter out of me, somehow. – I am better for being here but can't expect the effect to last long after I leave. – Give my love to all –
  Yours ever
    Edward Thomas

The 'good but difficult book of poems' was Lascelles Abercrombie's Interludes and Poems, *described more fully in a letter to Bottomley of the same date.*

[47]

Minsmere
28. ii. 08.

My dear Jesse,

I could manage to come on Tuesday just for the afternoon, at least I am almost sure; but on the other hand it is such a little while it would to me be worse than no time. Do you understand? I should feel all the afternoon that in an hour or so it will all be over. Therefore I won't come, which is selfish but I expect forgiven. Then we will look out for the earliest chance again. Should Helen & I be going to town by train stopping at Colchester then I will let you know & we can just look at one another for five minutes if you can get to the station. Goodbye.
  Ever yours
    Edward Thomas

[48]

> Berryfield Cottage,
> Ashford,
> Petersfield
> 8. viii. 08.

My dear Jesse,

As I am just going to be busier than ever I must send you a word to apologize for past & future neglect. I only sent off *Jefferies* early this week. I am already half way through another country book – to be called *The South Country*, & this & a life of Borrow have to be finished by Christmas. Added to these, I have just been appointed Assistant Secretary to a Royal Commission on Ancient Monuments in Wales, which may mean regular work at an office in Westminster beginning almost at once. How I shall ever do it all I don't know. I do nothing but work nowadays. Even when I take five days walking I fill notebooks all the time with observations & ideas. When I undertook all this work I thought it would be splendid getting so much out of myself: now I doubt & the well is not a bottomless one. However, when I am in town I ought to be able to get to Colchester – if you are still there. Are you? And how are you, & did Dell get into Christ's Hospital. I very much hope so. I am glad you liked Doughty. Of course he takes some getting into as any really new good man does. Perhaps you won't always call him rugged, though he is fine at rugged things. Now do please write again fairly soon & keep me up to the scratch. Helen has just gone away for a week's camping in Cornwall or she would send her love with mine to you all. We are all well, most of us very well, & *Helen says* I am better, & she ought to know.

Yours ever
Edward Thomas

<small>Charles Montagu Doughty (1845-1926) was the author of Travels in Arabia Deserta *(1888). Edward Garnett's recent abridgement of this, entitled* Wanderings in Arabia, *had been reviewed by ET in February.*</small>

[49]

> *Swansea*
> 14. xi. 08

My dear Jesse,

I ought to have written but now that I am on this Commission work I get no time & when I am not working I want to be out in the air. But I was hoping I might get down to you before Christmas. Is it possible? I suppose a weekend would be the worst time for you though. I didn't want to wait till strawberry time. Tell me.

And where is Frank(LYN)? I think of Dal very often, but he left a letter unanswered & so I have stupidly been silent.

We are well – Helen very busy for the Suffrage, actually making speeches. The children are as well as could be. As to me – I have a new excuse for grumbling in London & London air & noise & people. I escape & give up the Commission at Christmas.

Is *The Modern Child* out? If so I don't suppose I can get it, but if it is not I will try & get it.

I am down here walking about but handicapped by blisters now & at the moment uncomfortable & fidgety in a strange room with 2 clocks in it & longing to be at home or out of doors. This is a sublime horrible town among the mountains at the edge of the sea. No town fascinates me so much. It is very large but not like London, so large as to be incomprehensible as a whole. It is all furnaces, collieries, filth, stench, poverty & extravagant show, & the country & the sea at the very edge of it all.

My love to you all & mind you let me know when I can come down & then I will do my best to come soon.

Yours ever
    Edward Thomas

P.S. I brought your last letter down here meaning to write so credit me with that thought.

Jefferies is due for January or February. *Borrow* I have given up. *The South Country* is finished & due in the Spring.

> The Modern Child *was an anthology of poetry and prose by contemporary writers, including ET's friend Thomas Seccombe, to illustrate a liberal, post-Victorian, attitude to childhood; it was compiled by Hervey Elwes and published in November 1908. ET later resumed work on George Borrow, and published his study, subtitled 'The Man and his Books,' in 1912.*

[50]

Week Green
Petersfield
26. xii. 09

My dear Jesse,

I am glad to have drawn a letter from you. But I am so bad a letter writer myself now that I cannot complain of you who are probably busier. Nothing has happened that can easily be told since we had you with us except our move & that we are very glad of. The new house is very fine & it is dry & convenient & Mervyn said today when we were walking together that 'it seemed as if we had never lived at Berryfield.' Rags is still with us – a little older in body but not otherwise changed. I have done a lot of work but except reviews practically none of it has been published – a very short selection from it will be out in February uniform with *Horae Solitariae* – just half a dozen stories or sketches. The rest is too unpopular. In fact I seem to have reached a point where publishers will no longer pay me for books. They see I can't write books that will bring in big profits & I shall either have to cease to produce books or to do only what is asked for & that seems likely to be less & less. Dent had a hope I was going to turn out a popular & paying author but I hear that sales refute him. If only it were not next to impossible to turn back & live on less than one has been used to. However, I have been better on the whole this past year, & a little less irritable & depressed, though I have had bad periods & rheumatism worried me in the Spring. Both children were at Bedales last term as Helen was teaching there, but I don't know if Bronwen will manage the longer walk next term especially as Helen may be unable to teach – she is going to have another baby in the summer.

Ransome & his wife stayed on till the end of November, but have been away since, though their books &c are still here.

I will try to get over to Witham soon. But when you can come you know you will be welcome whatever the time: don't forget.

Helen & Mervyn & Bronwen & I send you all our love & good wishes.

Yours ever
Edward Thomas

Rags was a rough-haired terrier of great character, who is affectionately portrayed as 'Mike' in the posthumous collection Cloud Castle. *He had been with the family since the years at Elses Farm, where Arthur Ransome remembers walks with him* (Autobiography, *p. 87). Myfanwy Thomas recalls 'a very woolly bob-tailed dog, who was very beloved; he and I would curl up together and sleep, with me sucking the tip of his ear'.*

[51]
Wick [*Week* deleted] *Green,*
Petersfield
15. iii. 10

My dear Jesse,

This is only a word written sleepily at midnight to ask for the loan again of the book on Mysticism by Inge & also anything good on St Teresa & other mystics. I am to write a book on

Above All Saints' Vicarage, Witham
Left Jesse Berridge's house in Elsenham Street, Southfields, London

Maeterlinck & I want to know a lot more about mystics before I begin. I am going to be very busy, for I have another country book to do & a book on Women & English poets – the influence of women on English poets & the attitude of poets towards women. If you suggest any books or any line of thought I shall be very grateful, especially as I have to do the book in an even greater hurry than usual. I am loth to be doing so much in a hurry but there was no choice, unfortunately.

We are all well & most glad to have fine weather at last. We heard & saw the worst of the bad up here, I can tell you. Now we have been planting trees & sowing seeds. Helen is very well indeed & has been teaching at school again this term. How are you all now? I should like to come over for a day & a night soon, if I might. Tell me what is your best day if so & I will try to manage it. No hurry about the books. I shall have another of mine to give you when I see you next.

Yours ever with Helen's love & mine to Edna & yourself & the children.
   Edward Thomas

I forgot to thank you for your letter written in mid January, but I was very glad to have it.

ET amended his printed address to the local spelling. 'Week,' he told Bottomley, is 'merely an Ordnance Map offence'. The big red house in Cockshott Lane, on top of the hanger above Ashford, had been built for him by his Bedalian friend Geoffrey Lupton. The position seemed ideal at first, but it was exposed to the elements, and disillusionment soon set in (see ET's poems 'The New House' and 'Wind and Mist').

[52]
   Wick [*Week* deleted] *Green,*
   Petersfield
   14. iv. 10.

My dear Jesse,

It has just occurred to me you might answer an impertinent question I have just been putting to three other poets. It is to help me in my book on Women & Poets. I want to find out as many different ways as possible of establishing a relation between 'reality' and a poem to or about an individual woman. I want to know how & when poets write such poems, whether in the quiet of the end, of satiety, of anticipation, or of an interval in love's progress, or etc.. Well can you help me? Can you single out any poem of which you feel able to tell me the circumstances under which it was written & what relation it bears to 'reality' IF ANY, & if none then the nature of the fancy or whatever you think it might be called. If you can do this I will have your M.S. typed & return the original & I will ensure that nobody but myself has any suspicion of the authorship of the remarks, if I use them in any way. No matter how brief, or long, or obscure. Try.

Thank you for your letter. You must have had a good holiday with this change of wind unless it has brought you more rain than us. I hope you got plenty of sun. I fear you are not coming to us unless you take us by surprise today or tomorrow which we should be glad to see.

F. D. Maurice's book is one I might [   ] to see. Will you send it fairly soon?

With love from all of us

Yours ever
  Edward Thomas

ET omitted a word in the last sentence. F. D. Maurice's book was Mediaeval Philosophy *(1857).*

[53]

        Week Green,
        Petersfield
        10. vi. 10.

My dear Jesse,

I was afraid I never should send back your precious book simply because I did not find time to write you a word with it. As the time draws near for me to begin writing my book I get busier & busier, discovering new things to read, and I seem to get no thinking done at all. And I am only writing now because I am too sleepy to hold a book up. I get sleepy so easily, after reading some hundreds of pages of Byron's poems for example. Your book was a curious pleasure to read, I cannot tell you just how; and it was also useful, especially in the light of your letter. I could never have imagined, without being told by one who had done it, that a sonnet had been written *tête à tête* practically with the subject. And your account of this period, coinciding as it does with other M.S. & printed accounts I have been reading, has enlightened me a great deal.

Perhaps you will see the book some day, though at present my mind is so chaotic and distrustful that I can't see in the least what the book is going to be. If you can send me any opinions or suggestions – as you half promised to do when you wrote last, on May 9 – please do.

Now I must go & see what else I can do before sleeping. Forgive me for writing like this. I hope you are all well & not any the worse for the thunder & lightning or for the disloyal interruption of your vicar's sermons. With love to you all.

Yours ever
        Edward Thomas

Let me have a word to say your book has arrived safely through the post.

[54]
      Wick [*Week* deleted] *Green*
      Petersfield
      26. viii. 10.

My dear Jesse,

I am so sorry I did not write. Helen addressed a lot of postcards to send out after the event & did not do one for you & so I forgot too. It was 9 days ago now, another girl I am glad to say, & Helen & she have done very well from the start though the birth itself was a laborious one. You must come down & see her some day not too far off. As Leytonstone is nearer London I have one reason to be glad you are going there, But I hope it is not too crowded & unhealthy for you. Let me know when you are to move & I will certainly come over soon. I am just now not very busy & am very uncomfortable, wanting a holiday but not free to take it for some days more, & the weather is terrible for mind & body. I shall probably go to Wales for a week or ten days about Sept. 1 & then I have Maeterlinck to do. I finished 'Women & Poets' some days ago, not satisfactorily. It is the release from that job which makes me uneasy now. We are all well, Mervyn especially as he has had 4 weeks by the sea with the Hooton's at Minsmere. How are you all? Could you come over this Autumn & bring Dell with you? Please remember me to Edna & the naughty Denys & virtuous Christopher. I hope you have not been wanting your books back yet. There are one or two others you were going to lend me which I shall be ready for soon. With love from Helen Mervyn Bronwen & me

Yours ever
        Edward Thomas

Helen Elizabeth Myfanwy was born on August 16th. (ET preferred the 'phonetic' spelling of **Myvanwy** *and* **Mervyn**). *'Christopher' is ET's misnaming of JB's son Christian, for which he apologises in Letter 59.*

[55]

Wick Green,
Petersfield
8. xii. 10.

My dear Jesse,

I am very glad to hear from you at last. I wanted to send back your books but didn't know where. Now we must meet soon. If you are in town – or can be – on a Tuesday or Wednesday let me know & we will meet. I shall be up on the 20th & 21st I expect. I hope you have got a good open place to live in – I suppose you have, from what you say. Good luck to you in the new house & I shall come and see you in it before very long if you will have me. I am busy for a few weeks longer at Maeterlinck & pushing it through anyhow so long as it is finished. I could not make a good job of it so I am not going to hang about with it but just do the best I can in a short time. *Feminine Influence* came out 6 weeks ago & was killed by its price (10/6) & the Election. It was an interesting book but shockingly put together. I am very busy indeed now. We are all well, but in confusion because the school broke up a fortnight before its time on account of one case of scarlet fever, & here are the children & a foreign boy who was to spend the holidays with us, all indoors in the wet weather. However I can get to the study. Helen is nearly as well as ever now – not quite. The baby is Helen Elizabeth Myvanwy – I must tell you how to say Myvanwy, tho quite easy & obvious if you are not frightened by the look of it. She is very well & bright. I hope Edna is well & likes the change. We send our love to you
  Yours ever
     Edward Thomas

<small>The new house: the Berridge family had moved to Norton House, High Stone, Leytonstone, and JB was now curate at St Luke's, Leyton. The Election: a rare reference in ET's letters to a political event; the general election in this month confirmed H. H. Asquith's Liberal ministry in power.</small>

[56]

Wick Green,
Petersfield
[mid-January 1911]

My dear Jesse,

Here are your books which I meant to have sent before with my thanks. Thanks too from Helen Elizabeth Myvanwy for the Boy Scout which she sometimes sucks at. How are you all? Can't we meet in town before long? If you are ever in town on a Tuesday between 4 & 6 come to St. George's: I am there every other

Tuesday mostly. If not let us meet somehow. You are not far away & if you don't come to us I shall come to you. We are all well. But I have just finished Maeterlinck; a dirty job I regret to say. I am going off for two or three days to wipe away some of the dirt.

With our love
Ever yours
    Edward Thomas

[57]

Wick Green,
Petersfield
Christmas 1911

My dear Jesse,

Why have you waited till now to write? Was that silly afternoon we spent enough to last a year? It was not for me, & I was hoping again & again to see you at St. George's or hear of you, but in vain. However I have been away a great deal travelling on the old road from Thetford to near Swindon which I have written a book about, & then latterly staying in Wales for over 2 months because my state of mind had got really much worse. I am just back & I think better. I shall be still better when I hear from you especially if you are all as well as I hope you are. Helen & I & Mervyn & Bronwen send you our all. Myvanwy who is now 16 months does not know you yet, which is your fault. Tell me if you are ever in town.

I would have sent Dell a book as usual but the fact is this has been a very bad year for me & I did not spend anything at all on Christmas presents & as no suitable book for him was to be found I left him unsaluted & was perhaps sorrier than he, for I am sure he is getting too old to submit to other people's choice of books.

I am writing a book on Pater. Tell me what to say or not to say or ask some questions.

Yours ever
    Edward Thomas

[58]

Wick Green,
Petersfield
16. i. 12.

My dear Jesse,

I put away your letter so safely that I cannot find it, though

I daily look through my pockets for it. So I shall write without being sure that I am not being very negligent & crass. I am not going to argue about 'the stile' and the *anima naturaliter Christiana* of its unreverend hero. But don't label me a.n.c. while I am alive. It seems so particularly a privilege of the unresisting dead to have someone come down upon them & pin that order onto their breasts. It won't matter then.

When you said you had been ill I was sorry. When you said you had been to the Isle of Wight I was sorrier because you had not come by the L.S.W.R. & stopped here on your way. But I am too old now to ask you to say why you didn't. Still, remember Petersfield is our station, that this chilly heart is at least no chillier. Well, where shall we meet? If you were to be at St. George's next Tuesday at 4 I would be there also; or I could probably manage lunch on Wednesday if that would be better. But tea is a better time don't you think?

(Did I tell you I am going to write a book on Pater? If I do I expect I shall offer it to you.)

I am usually up every other Monday or Tuesday so if next week doesn't suit you tell me what day will. We all send our love to you all. I wish I could find that letter.

Yours ever
    Edward Thomas

L.S.W.R.: *the London & South Western Railway, which became part of the newly amalgamated Southern Railway in 1921. When* Walter Pater *was published in 1913, the dedication was to Joseph Conrad.*

[59]

13 Rusham Rd.
Balham S.W.
19. iii. 12.

My dear Jesse,

I apologise for the burden I have been laying on Christian's shoulders, & hope he has not felt it too heavy. I am sending in the dedication.

I can't promise the 27th. I am going to walk about Warwickshire & Gloucestershire & should the weather turn fine I might stay on past the 27th. But if you can keep it open I will let you know *if I can come.*

Pater is roughly finished but I shall keep it by me for suggestions till after Easter.

Yours ever
    Edward Thomas

Edward Thomas in 1913

[59a]

Wick Green,
Petersfield
22. vii. 12.

Dear Mrs. Berridge,
 This is the book I meant for you and the children. Will you accept it and forgive me for misspelling Dennis? If you won't for-

give me then I won't forgive Jesse for not coming here or seeing me in London. And how are you all and did you enjoy the Spring? We did, though most of the time I was away in solitude writing a book. Helen sends her love with mine to you and Jesse and all.

Sincerely yours
        Edward Thomas

[59b]

Wick Green,
Petersfield
23. vii. 12.

My dear Mrs. Berridge,

Thank for your letter. I was relieved to hear I had not made Denys out of Dennis as I thought. If you enjoy any of these old tales which I have rearranged and retold, I shall be very glad: or if you don't perhaps Denys will. I wish I could come down to see you this week end and it is most kind of you to ask me. But we are expecting several visitors on Sunday, and after that for a month I have engagements which will keep me here or still further from you. Early in September or late in August if you are free will be a better time for me: or perhaps I had better wait until Dell is back at school. I hope Jesse is well though so busy. We all send our love to you.

Yours sincerely,
        Edward Thomas

NOTE by Jesse Berridge. *'The title page of* Norse Tales *in my possession indicates it was published at Oxford, Clarendon Press, in 1912. The printed Dedication runs "For Edna, Jesse, Dell, Denys, Christian and Wilfrid Berridge," with the autograph writing added "with love from Edward Thomas, 22. vii. 12." (Mr Eckert's* Bibliography *seems inaccurate here).'*

[60]

Wick Green
27. viii. 12.

My dear Jesse,

I am glad you wrote but wish you had better news. What a pity you can't come down to Elses Farm & have warm weather & fish for tench. Here there are no tench & no warm weather & time makes other differences. But I have no grumbles against you except that you didn't arrange to meet long ago. I forget when I wrote last, but it was since I got back from *Swinburne* & Wiltshire, I think. *Pater* I finished in March. Since *Swinburne* I have

had very little to do & still have bad prospects, so that it seems likely we shall leave here before a year is out, though we want to make sure of good schools before moving. Can you particularly recommend any day school not in London? I was bicycling with Mervyn past Horsham & thought of you & Dell & the school there. Perhaps it would be possible for us. Meantime I have to look out for a regular job of some kind. Books won't keep me any longer: that seems certain. But I am glad you liked the Norse Tales. I don't know quite when I can come to you, probably some time in September. My visits to town are now fewer & more irregular but we might meet in about a fortnight's time if you could be up then. Let me know your best day. Monday or Thursday would suit me best for lunch Any day would do for tea. I hope you will have better news by then & everybody better weather. It is a fine night now & the day was at any rate rainless. Good luck to you & all of yours. With our love to you
    Ever yours
        Edward Thomas

JB's eldest son, Dell, now aged 16, was at school at Christ's Hospital, Horsham. He was ET's favourite among the Berridge boys; the family still has the inscribed copy of Richard Jefferies' Bevis *which ET gave him.*

[61]

Dillybrook Farm,
Road, nr Bath
14. ii. 13.

My dear Jesse,

Thank you. I had been meaning to write. But things have been very wrong & I couldn't. I have now come away bicycling & go today for a week with Clifford Bax at the Manor House, Broughton Gifford, Wilt. So I am not sure I can see the Russians' show. If I am up in time – & I might be on the 25th – I will let you know. In any case, show or not, we can meet soon.

We have now definitely arranged to leave our house in June & go to a cottage near the school. We look forward to the move as to a chance of salvation. But I know too well that something else will be necessary besides a move. My health is now definitely bad – not mere depression – & I don't know how it will develop. I thought it was lack of exercise but the last few days show that I am scarcely fit for much exercise. However if the sun were to reappear it might make a difference.

I hope you weren't horribly tired the day after *Cinderella* & weren't asked 'who were you with last night' too seriously. I was

up the next week with Bronwen at a children's party & have been no good since. Goodbye. I hope the children's ailments have not been very bad for them & Edna & you. With love
    Yours ever
        Edward Thomas

   Clifford Bax (1886-1962) was later well-known as a dramatist. ET stayed with him frequently at Broughton Gifford and at 11 Luxemburg Gardens, Hammersmith; it was through him that ET first met Eleanor Farjeon in 1912. The Russians' show: both Edward and Helen Thomas loved the ballet. Thomas Beecham was presenting a winter season of grand opera and Russian Ballet at Covent Garden. Cinderella *was one of the season's pantomimes, at the Princes Theatre (where seats cost from 1/6 to 5/-).*

[62]
           Wick Green,
           (after tomorrow)
           6. v. 13.

My dear Jesse,
    Thank you very much, & I should be glad to have the 1d. mission books & also the loan yet again of Inge's *Christian Mysticism* & of any other book, such as St Theresa, which will help me to know more about religious rapture & ecstasy – Plotinus in translation, for example. I am going home tomorrow for a while so if you will send the books there I shall be grateful.
    Yes we will do another ride or walk, if I cure my blisters. I have been working too much to keep fit since, & mostly in London. Things will not clear up in spite of dates & nuts.
    With my love
    Yours ever
        Edward Thomas

   ET had been staying in London, at Martin Freeman's flat at 166 Lauderdale Mansions, Maida Vale; he was working on In Pursuit of Spring, *an account of a bicycle journey across the south of England on which JB had accompanied him in March. He was also considering a short book on the subject of Ecstasy (see Letter 64 & note).*

[63]
           Wick Green,
           Petersfield
           [*undated*: early June 1913]

My dear Jesse,
    We hope to move this month & I have been clearing up & destroying. I had a vast collection of M.S.S. which are now in a

much more useful condition in the form of ashes. But this MS of *The Heart of England* is so neat I couldn't burn it. It occurred to me you might like to shelter it for a few years longer until you have a clearing up. I am selling a large proportion of my books. Are any of those on this list worth buying? Except the Yeats and Symonds they will go for 1/6 to 2/6 a volume. Please return the list whenever you write.

And thank you for the books you sent. I am now typing 4000 words a day at my book. Should I be able to get to town next week which time & day suits you best? I will try to manage it. Helen's in town with baby. I'm alone, very much so.

With love to you all
Yours ever
Edward Thomas

This letter accompanied the MS of The Heart of England *both when ET sent the MS to Jesse Berridge and when the latter presented it, through the Edward Thomas Memorial Committee, to the National Museum of Wales in 1936. ET also sent Gordon Bottomley a list of the books he was selling, on 9 June. The book he was now typing would have been either* In Pursuit of Spring *or his novel* The Happy-Go-Lucky Morgans.

[64]

Steep [Wick Green *deleted*],
Petersfield
[*about* 25. 7. 13.]

My dear Jesse,

It can be managed. Will you come down on Wednesday by the *fast train* leaving Waterloo at 9 & cycle on with Mervyn & me to Goodwood racecourse (if fine), where we shall join Helen & Bronwen? We can give you a bed. Then we will fix up Thursday & Friday later. Or of course come on Tuesday night if you can. We moved on Tuesday & are now straight. All is pretty well except that I have no work, tho I am still considering the subject of Ecstasy for a little book & we can talk it over, if you like. Send me a card to say what you will do. With our love & looking forward very much to seeing you.

Yours & Edna's ever,
Edward Thomas

The move was to 2 Yew Tree Cottages, in a group of six new semi-detached 'artisans' dwellings' in the village of Steep. ET's little book on Ecstasy for Batsford's 'Fellowship Books' got no further than a typescript (now in the Berg Collection in the New York Public Library, but undated). The previous year he had contributed The Country *to this new series, for which Eleanor Farjeon wrote* Trees *and Clifford Bax* Friendship.

[65]

Steep
23. ii. 14.

My dear Jesse,

I ought to have written at once, but the fact is I was busy with some odd jobs & very impatient to begin my book. That was 3 days ago. I meant to begin today but simply couldn't even begin to try to begin. So at the end of the day's writing I will write about your suggestion. When I first read it I felt it to be very much impossible, because I had given up that story. I talked it over with several people, including two novelists, & thought I had got it clear, whereas I had really only got it clear enough to see the difficulties. So I was intending to attempt a totally different story. Now I should like to collaborate with you. Should I succeed in getting to work on the *second* story of course I must go on with it. But if I don't I shall be very glad to hear what your idea is. Or had we better wait till I am up next, in a fortnight or so? I ought to warn you by the way that I didn't mean the lovers to be platonic & they were to get married in a hurry just to make their walking tour respectable – they were regarding that week as their last week of perfect freedom, before entering on their parts in middle class existence. If you want them to remain chaste, do you intend to ignore the sexual side or to assume that they are capable of ignoring it? In a whole book on a honeymoon there must be some sex unless the thing is lightest comedy.

After this do you feel inclined to tell me how far the idea had gone in your mind? In any case you didn't really imagine that you could be capable of cheek to me or I of perceiving it in you, did you?

Our love to you all, & when are you coming down to *fetch your lamp*?

Yours ever
  Edward Thomas

 The book which ET was impatient to begin was his autobiography, eventually published in 1938 as The Childhood of Edward Thomas. *Nothing came of the proposed literary collaboration with JB.*

[66]

Steep,
Petersfield
3. v. 14.

My dear Jesse,

I ought to have sent you this account of our journey before, but

I have been away with the children in Wales and Herefordshire and am only just back. You mustn't give away the fact that the Other Man is rather a lie. Things go on much the same, but I keep myself busy. I have done something daily at Edition, so that it has grown in stature. But I don't like it and have had thoughts of stopping halfway, and should do so were there anything else to occupy me.

We are all well and I hope you are. I haven't been much in town for a month or more. When I am next up I hope we can meet. Are you all well? We send our love to you.

Yours ever
Edward Thomas

This S. Teresa is yours, isn't it?

This letter was enclosed with a copy of In Pursuit of Spring. *JB was ET's cycling companion on the second half of the journey from London to the coast of Somerset which is described in the book. In a letter to E. S. P. Haynes enclosed with a copy of the same book in 1921, ET's brother Julian wrote: 'I accompanied Edward from Balham to Salisbury Plain in the making of it'. He also refers to the journey in his sonnet 'In Memoriam: E.T.' 'Edition': probably the collection of articles on the 'homes and haunts' of English writers, eventually published in 1917 as* A Literary Pilgrim in England.

[67]

Steep,
Petersfield
3. ix. 14.

My dear Jesse,

How are you all now? I should have written. Now we have left Herefordshire, Helen & the children for home, I for a week or so in the Midlands & the North on a little job, one of my last for some time I expect. I don't quite know what will happen. The obvious thing is to join the Territorials but I can't leave other people to keep my family till I know I can't do it myself. What do you say? I am slowly growing into a conscious Englishman. I hope your holiday was only disturbed by papers once a day. We did well on the whole. Mervyn had some dull days but he went off to friends near for a week & cycled home over the ground we 3 covered & they are all at Steep now. I hope we are to be allowed to visit Avebury one day & to meet long before that, perhaps this month. At this moment I am in Coventry on my way to Sheffield Manchester & Newcastle. Give my love to Edna & the children.

Yours ever
Edward Thomas

Right The Thomases' house on Bearsted Green
Below No 2 Yew Tree Cottages, Steep

The Thomas family had been staying at a farmhouse at Ledington, near Ledbury, close to the cottage rented by Robert Frost. (For a full account of the holiday, see Eleanor Farjeon's Edward Thomas: The Last Four Years*). The 'little job' entailed a fortnight's rail journey from Swindon to Newcastle, via Coventry, Birmingham, Sheffield and Manchester, on which ET gathered material for an article on what people were saying about the war which had just begun, and its effects, with some reflections on patriotism. It was published as 'Tipperary' in the* English Review *in October, and reprinted in* The Last Sheaf *in 1928.*

[68]

Steep
6. i. 15.

My dear Jesse,

Will you please thank Dell for his letter to me & excuse me from writing to you both because I am laid up for a time with a sprained ankle & writing is not easy. But it is getting on well enough, thank you.

I expect I have to congratulate you on your move to Brentwood, as it must mean you have got the job you were telling me about. I am very glad indeed, & shall be gladder if it means you can come here for longer visits & makes Avebury as certain as possible. It looks as if I shall remain in England all the year unless the war ends soon. If only you could come down to give me Christian consolation in my (moderate) distress! also to talk about England. I am writing an article on what England means to people. I wonder could you give me any thoughts you have had, the more intimate & purely your own the better, – any thoughts symbolising England by any particular places, persons, events, or words. I don't ask for an essay because I don't want so much to know what you can think if you set yourself to as what you habitually or instinctively or at some special moment have felt. A short note would help, as I am prevented now while the essay is being prepared from seeing & sending to anybody as I had intended. I have no other work, but haven't begun to worry yet, as I find I can go on doing work I want to do though nobody else wants me to. I have even begun to write verse, but don't tell a soul, as if it is to be published at all it must be anonymously.

A happy 1915 to you & Edna & all.
Yours ever
      E.T.

JB had moved to Rosslyn, Rose Valley, Brentwood, to take up the post of chaplain to the Essex County Asylum. ET's first poem, 'Up in the Wind,' had been completed on 3 December 1914.

[69]

Steep,
Petersfield
25. v. 15.

My dear Jesse,

It is just 2 months since you wrote & I haven't written back, chiefly because there didn't seem much chance of seeing you yet. I have been in town a little but only to work at the Museum. I have had no excursions. For I don't feel very free to spend & just about the end of March I began a new piece of work, a life of Marlborough. After 6 or 7 weeks reading I began the writing last week & it will keep me close at it for I don't quite know how long, but less than 2 months I hope. Then I shall be free or empty & have to make up my mind what to do if there isn't any work. I tried to get a job at the historical section of the War Office, but only had my name put down on possibly a very long list.

It looks as if the anniversary of our last journey together will not fall in a time of peace. But I may be able & inclined to take another journey. Is it possible you will? I am still suffering from my ankle or perhaps I should regard some military service as the thing for me especially if ordinary work fails. Nobody that I know well has enlisted so I am really at sea as to how men really feel about it & if my own hesitations are at all common.

I should like to hear what Dell has done. He had just been recommended for a commission when you wrote.

Mervyn seems farther off now. He has settled down happily & from the tone of his letters & the accounts he gives of riding & fishing & making a waterwheel &c I think he must have almost wakened up as I hoped he would. But when he will come back is uncertain.

It has been a most lovely Spring here. We had a nightingale singing close to the house for 3 weeks. I have gone on with my versification & I will send you some specimens with this, & I should like to know if you find anything to like among them. For the time being I am shut up, I think, by the work I have in hand. I have sent some out to all the possible papers &c without success & the only publisher who would have kept the secret – I wanted to use a pseudonym – is quite unfavourable.

Let me have some news & tell me if you can ever meet me in town though just now I am not proposing to be up much.

With my love to you all
Yours ever
Edward Thomas

Mervyn Thomas sailed with the Frosts to the United States on 16 February, to stay with his former headmaster in New Hampshire; he returned in December. It is unfortunately impossible to know which of his poems ET sent for JB's inspection; he had by now written some seventy-five – just over half of the Collected Poems *(ed. R. George Thomas, 1978).*

[70]

Steep,
Petersfield
1. vi. 15.

My dear Jesse,

I am very glad to get your news. Of course my verses would not be good reading for you if you are reading the papers a lot. There's the difference. I can't read them. I wait for them & then when they come I am through them in five minutes standing up ready to go up the hill & do a great slab of Marlborough. Well I think I can end it in 3 full weeks & so be free for you. 1 ride would clear my head best I think, if it suits you. We could go to Avebury & up round. I don't know how many days you will spare. But I have an engagement in Gloucester about that time & we might end up there. You could come here for a night, or else we could meet at Reading say. Of course I can't swear I shall be done, but I really think so if things go on as they do. Stuart Reid's book was no good.

I am so glad you like your garden & hope you have really got your ears back again now. And it is good news that Dell gets on & enjoys it. I hope he will do well. Give him my love.

Send the verses back when you have done with them. I fancy they are sufficiently new in their way to be unacceptable if the reader gets caught up by their way & doesn't get any effect before he begins to consider & see their 'unfinish'.

Yours ever with our love to you all

Edward Thomas

The news which ET was glad to get was probably of JB's appointment to the parish of Little Baddow. The bicycle tour took place in the second half of the month. JB accompanied ET as far as Stroud, via Southampton, Avebury and Malmesbury. In Gloucester, ET stayed with his friend John Haines, a solictor and skilled amateur botanist, whom he had met through Robert Frost and Lascelles Abercrombie the previous summer.

[71]

[*written in pencil*]

13 Rusham Rd.,
Balham S.W.
13. xi. [1915]

My dear Jesse,

How are you and how is Dell? I have had 5 weeks in camp

when it was not possible to get to you, but now we are off to a new camp near Romford I look forward to getting over to Brentwood. It is not certain that I shall be free to go off by train during the week, but in case I can will you tell me what are your freest evenings. I could probably give you a day's warning·

Since I saw you I have almost completed my training except that my musketry course was cut short. I am now having a change, acting as an instructor in map-reading & map-making, & am exalted to be a lance-corporal. This will delay my commission a little but I do not expect to remain an instructor for ever.

Write a word to my Balham address whence it will be forwarded. I do not yet know precisely what my camp address will be.

We are all well, especially myself, & all looking forward to having Mervyn with us at Steep for Christmas.

I do hope you have only good news. Tell me soon & give my love to Edna and the boys.

Yours ever
Edward Thomas

<small>The five weeks were spent in camp at High Beech in Epping Forest, close to the semi-detached nurseryman's house to which the family moved in October 1916.</small>

[72]

[*Postcard, written in pencil. Postmarked* Romford 2.30 a.m. 30 Nov. 15.; *addressed to* Rev. J. Berridge, Rosslyn, Rose Valley, Brentwood.]

>4229
>A. *Company,*
>*Artists Rifles,*
>*Harehall Camp,*
>*nr Romford*

I am going to try to get over tomorrow at teatime unless it is very wet.
E.T.

[73]

[*On YMCA printed paper,* H.M. Forces on Active Service.]

>*Steep is the best address now*
>12. vi. 16.

My dear Jesse,

It has not been possible to get to you. Things have altered altogether in the Artists. I have now offered myself for the Artillery, been accepted, & am expecting shortly to leave for training which may begin at St John's Wood barracks. I am delighted with the idea of a change. This is not the only one. Mervyn is going as an apprentice on Sept. 4 to engineering works at Blackhorse Lane, Walthamstow, & we are going to move to High Beech or somewhere not too far off. You don't happen to know of a cottage or a (more or less) rural neighbourhood that might suit us? What you might know is a place near Leytonstone where Mervyn could lodge and board for a few weeks before we move. If you should know somebody would you ask them to write to Helen? I suppose he would be out from 8.30 till 6 or perhaps from 6 till 6.

I wonder if you still have good news of Dell? Are you ever at Romford now or is it ever possible for you to come over to Hare Hall Camp (I am at Hut 3) on a Saturday for example. We no longer have Wednesdays. Any evening would do. I am here on leave till Wednesday. Helen & the children send their love to you all & so do I.

Ever yours
(*Cpl*) *P. E. Thomas*

JB was now Rector of Little Baddow, near Chelmsford. His son Dell had left King's College, London, where he was a chemistry student, to join the Royal Engineers; he was now serving as a lieutenant at the Front.

[74]

*13 Rusham Rd,
Balham,
London S.W.
17. ix. 16*

My dear Jesse,

I have been a most unconscionable time, but I do thank you for sending me those addresses. Through Mrs — at Walthamstow, who couldn't take him herself, we got rooms for Mervyn which he has now been in two weeks & likes very well. We move at or near the end of this month to High Beech. 'Paul's Nursery, High Beech, Loughton' will find us. This address is best for me. I am at the moment at Steep, but I have been 3 weeks in barracks at Handel St nr Russell Square & am expecting to be moved shortly to Trowbridge. There I may be gazetted. The work is not easy for me especially as I have been out of sorts altogether since July when I was vaccinated: still I may get through. I am not enjoying this half & half cadet stage a bit.

Everyone is well, tho we are all scattered till the moving is over. Helen alone is here. She sends her love with mine to you all.

Edward Thomas in uniform of the Artists' Rifles

If I don't go to Trowbridge this week – I was going to suggest a 24 hour weekend with you: but that is the worst time for you isn't it? And you are never in town after 6 p.m. when I am free, are you? Suggest anything you can.
   Yours ever
        Edward Thomas

The lady at Walthamstow is not named. ET was gazetted as a second-lieutenant, Royal Garrison Artillery, on 20 November.

[75]

244th Siege Battery,
R.A. Mess,
Tintown,
Lydd, Kent
24. xii. 16.

My dear Jesse,

I am now one of the 3 junior subalterns in this battery which expects to go out with 9.2 inch howitzers in a month or so. That is pretty well all the news. I was gazetted 2nd Lt. last month & have been busy ever since doing a final course & getting into the work of the battery. We are a very mixed lot of officers & I wonder how we are going to amalgamate. I get on fairly well & I like Romney Marsh. Twice I have seen Conrad who lives 12 miles away. We are all well at home. Mervyn gets on at his work & likes it. He is brighter & happier than he was. Bronwen goes to Loughton to school. Myvanwy keeps Helen company. And how are you all? Above all, how is Dell? My best wishes & love to you. When I get mobilization leave I hope I can come over to you or you to me.

Yours ever
Edward Thomas

Joseph Conrad (1857-1924) was living at this time at Capel House, Orlestone, near Ashford, Kent. Many years later Mrs Conrad wrote: 'Edward Thomas appeared to me always as the quintessence of gentleness'.

[76]

[*headed paper, corrected in ink.*]   *R.A. Mess,*
Tin [*Hut* deleted] *Town,*
Lydd
3. i. 17.

My dear Jesse,

We are soon going. We are shooting this week & mobilizing next – we go to Codford on Salisbury Plain on the 13th. Meantime I should have leave & I will try to come over with Helen for one day. Let me know how we get from Chelmsford. A night, I think, is impossible.

I am so glad you have only good news of Dell. To be slightly wounded sounds good news.

My love to all of you & I hope we shall meet.

Yours ever
    Edward Thomas

[77]

High Beech
Tuesday [9. 1. 17.]

My dear Jesse,

I hope you are not expecting us today. I meant to come, but I did not hear from you, & then I had a very bad night last night & the morning was stormy & these things just unfixed my resolution, especially as I did not know at all whether you would be at home or free. If you were & especially if you were expecting us, please forgive me, & unless I am to see you in town I must say goodbye. I may have some free time at Codford but no leave. After the end of the month I shall be found by this address

    2/Lt: P. E. Thomas
    244 Siege Battery
    B.E.F.
    France

My love & greetings to Edna & the children.

Yours ever
    Edward Thomas

Though ET was never able to visit the Berridges at Little Baddow Rectory, his Diary records 'tea with Jesse and T. Clayton' on 11 January. This, their last meeting, took place in London. Four days later, Edward Thomas left Lydd to mobilise with his battery at Codford on Salisbury Plain; he embarked with them at Southampton for Le Havre on 29 January, never to return. He was killed near Arras on 9 April 1917.

Edward

A Memoir by Jesse Berridge

> That girl's clear eyes utterly concealed all
> Except that there was something to reveal.
> And what did mine say in the interval?
> No more: no less. They are but as a seal
> Not to be broken till after I am dead;
> And then vainly.

It is perhaps a question whether all we write about Edward shall serve to reveal much of the secret of his personality. We break the seal, but the manuscript within is in the form of our own memories. Our contributions of little pieces of worked and coloured stone make a mosaic and attempt a portrait, but at best the result must needs have a sort of Byzantine quality, an emphasis on externals, decorative, literary, with a consequent remoteness. The English words that did indeed choose him for his deep love of them seem in lesser hands such as mine to fall far short of letting him

> Stand perchance
> In ecstasy
> Fixed and free

nor at our bidding will he 'pace forth' for those who come after us, and even as I write I seem to hear his laughter at my allusions and solemnity.

Last night – I am writing in the Spring of 1947 – I dreamed vividly of Edward. In my dream he was coming down a road, in loose dark clothes, to meet me, with his long purposeful stride and his face alight with pleasure and gaiety. Well I knew that look on his face, and here and now I would give my testimony that I did know very many hours in his company, and in by far the greater part of them he was happy, sometimes with an almost bewildering intensity. It is true I have been with him in moods of despondency, even hidden resentment (never with me in all our friendship) and I have shared silence with him in some times of depression that yet were transient, and of great disappointment borne courageously. I had really, so far as I know, so little to give him in return for that supreme gift of his friendship except affection and the open and expressed fact that I was happy in his company, and it seemed at the time just what he wanted. He is taking his place among the immortals, and I would deprecate over-emphasis on the darker side of his unique personality, such as is suggested by some portraits of him.

My literary interests and immature efforts were remote from his supreme vision and ability in expression, and served, if they served at all, in making evident his wonderful kindliness and his appreciation of what then meant much to me. To write of him now daunts me. Yet in one of his letters to me he was asking for any thoughts I had on a certain subject. 'I don't ask for an essay, because I don't want too much to know what you can think if you set yourself to, as what you habitually or instinctively or at some special moment have felt.' So in this my poor gift to his memory I will not attempt the path of biography, that has been already well travelled, nor can anything be added to Mr de la Mare's splendid appreciation of his work, but add my stray memories of what I can recall across the years, of the momentous experience of his friendship.

It was in 1901 that I first met Edward at Duncan Williams's flat in Gray's Inn Road. He was just down from Oxford, and joined in the talk of our voluble and amusing circle at intervals, rather remote, kindly, giving the impression of reserves of knowledge, of perhaps a suppressed anxiety. He was living then at Nightingale Parade, Balham. I went to his rooms there and found the atmosphere of friendliest welcome and sincere pleasure at my visit, to which Helen's hospitality and affectionate character contributed so much. I knew instinctively that by intimacy with him I should find one of the best gifts that life has to offer. So subsequently I found, and until I saw him for the last time when he was in camp near Romford and came to see us at our home in Brentwood, I loved and admired him and was ever happy in his company, stimulated to be at my best in sincerity and speech. It was not, I think, chiefly his culture and literary conversation, nor merely his finished and expressive talk, grave humour and beautiful voice, but a strange undaunted honesty in his judgements, an impatience with what was meretricious or superficial in people and things and social arrangements, and a profound love of the simple and the natural, that bound me to him.

As our friendship progressed he would at times call for me in the City at the Bank where I was employed, and his unusual appearance, his fine face, light hair, and clothes that told of a rural life, made a strange contrast to all of us in that restless and commercial environment. I think even then those of us who knew him well might have prophesied his distinction as a poet. His extreme sensitiveness, love of common things and vision of their value and significance, his growing mastery of words and fastidious selection of them, his ear for the music of a phrase as evidenced in his writings, should have indicated the direction his developed powers would take. The early impact of anxiety and the responsibility for others must have deepened and strengthened him, but only on looking back does one feel this to be true. He had much suffering to endure before he found serenity and poise as the happy warrior and the major poet.

We made a number of excursions together, taking bicycles and putting up haphazard at inns – Avebury, Swindon, Malmesbury, Stroud, Westbury, Bridgwater, Selborne and other places. One of these journeys is recorded in a book he wrote, *In Pursuit of Spring*, though the 'other man' referred to in it as his companion is 'rather a fraud', as he wrote to me in sending me the volume. As an illustration of his extraordinary talent for giving an intense significance to a single, almost momentary, experience, I recall on that occasion lying on the beach at Kilve. We had confirmed the fact that there was no weathercock on the church,[1] and were resting in peace and almost in silence. Then he turned and bade me listen. A little melodious twitter sounded somewhere, and a tiny bird dipped and swooped between us and the sea. 'A meadow pipit,' he said, and the moment became unforgettable. But indeed, he made all things lightly passed over or unnoticed to possess a value only perceived when he made us see with something of the vision he himself possessed. I hold it to be the spiritual value, and whether he would have acknowledged the word or no, there was something of the mystic in his poet's vision. His poems contain ample illustration of this feeling then awakened in me that I now 'remember in tranquillity'. He would cut out walking-sticks from the wood and shape them until they had a character of their own. A knife of mine at least sixty years old, formerly belonging to my father, with a long bone handle so worn with the hand that the white showed through the outer part, had a peculiar fascination for him; somehow I saw it had a soul that his view of it had created.

1. In Pursuit of Spring, *p. 282; also* The South Country, *p. 6, where ET writes: 'Politics, the drama, science, . . . I cannot grasp; . . . when they are discussed I am given to making answers like, "In Kilve there is a weathercock".' (Editor's note.)*

Jesse Berridge about 1918

He delighted in sea-songs or shanties I remembered from hearing them sung by the sailors, when as a child I went to Australia in 1882 in a sailing-ship with my father, who commanded her. If a song was new to Edward he would get me to sing it over and over while he learned it, and Helen would sit at the piano and jot down the notes. He loved singing – old songs, racy songs, songs that had won the acceptance of a robust democracy as a permanent possession, songs of Tudor fragility and daintiness – but he limited his audience to a family circle. I never heard of him singing or making a speech in public. He would perch a small child on his knee, and clasp his clay pipe with his fine strong hands, and the music that was in him would come forth, wistfully or jauntily. My children delighted in his too rare visits. 'Leg-over-leg,' they would demand, and he would comply with the jingle about the fox.[2]

I suppose I was just bookish enough to trail some way with him in his literary work and interests, but it was companionship he needed mostly of me, I think. 'Your letter was more to me than praise, and I know you meant it to be, only just now such friendships as yours makes me feel the bitterness of my isolation more.' So he wrote. I suppose I have kept about seventy letters from him, and in the greater part of them there is a suggestion for a meeting or an invitation. 'A three-mile walk tires me just as much as 30 miles with a friend.'

I have referred to him somewhat hesitatingly as a mystic. He would, I think, have shied at the word; and yet one cannot fail to catch the authentic note in some of his poems – at the close of 'Lights Out', for instance, or in that thrilling lyric 'After You Speak'. In his prose work, too, there is so frequently a reminder of this. His own nature reacted to a certain religious chord in the make-up of others, though all who knew him knew how he hated the smug, the pretentious, the self-opinionated, the merely officially religious, and the hardness that sometimes accompanies piety. He was curious about my resolve to take Orders, but I never remember being wounded by anything he said. He was curious too about the mysticism of Richard Jefferies. I have a copy of Behmen Edward gave me, and a Crashaw. He asked me to procure for him St Theresa's writings, the *Imitation*, the *Vulgate*, and borrowed Inge's *Christian Mysticism* several times. He rejected emphatically the easy label of *anima naturaliter Christiana*. 'Don't label me a. n. c. while I am alive. It seems so particularly a privilege of the unresisting dead to have someone come down

2. *Leg over leg / As the fox went to Dover / When he came to a stile / Hop! – he went over.* (Editor's note.)

upon them and pin that order on their breasts. It can't matter then.' Still, he had written earlier, 'Among my unfertilised plans still lies an Essay on the Gospel of St John by a Devout Agnostic.'

I remember longing greatly that he should experience some awareness of God, especially when I learned that he had turned to expressing himself in poetry. He told me of his poems and sent me some in 1915. I may have said something about there being only one cure for his melancholia. He wrote back to say he did not know what I meant. But I still feel that his interest in mysticism was something much more than an effort towards a literary understanding of Jefferies and Maeterlinck. He had the most exquisite expression of thought of any man I ever knew, but there was something in him ever inexpressible. And the merely romantic side of supernatural experience repelled him, particularly when it took literary expression. He once entertained the idea of collaborating with me in a novel, but his honesty, and recognition of the imperatives in his own experience and outlook, would not coalesce with my rather pretentious idealism, and the idea came to nothing.

I have said that as I knew him he was mostly happy, and I can recall many hours of talk, of sitting up at night to go fishing at dawn, hours at Goodwood, at the pantomime even, when life seemed to him something intensely good; but all his intimates have experienced that other side of him, and how sombre it was. I remember telling him, because I found his complexity baffling, that he was 'devious'; humbly, and without irony, he accepted the description. He was on one occasion in the depths of depression, and I began to have a real fear that his morbidity might affect his reason. He had an idea that he had diabetes, and was obsessed with a story he had heard that sufferers from that disease grew so hungry that they ate earth. In imagination he saw himself in that dire condition, and yet the mood passed swiftly as we talked, and he swung quickly to an almost boisterous hilarity over a song that we both knew, of dubious decency, with variations and glosses. His sense of the ridiculous often approached hysteria to my sober view, and it was very catching.

I do not know what more about Edward can be added by me that has not been written elsewhere and better. If I have put in a few touches to the record of the man, which may help to give a clearer idea of how his fine and troubled spirit made life a lovelier thing to one friend, and of the capacity for splendid and generous companionship which that spirit included, I have not written in vain.

Impressions more subtle than those created by ordinary perception remain, when memories of hearing and seeing blur with the years. I repeat that, as I knew him, laughter and joy made up far more of his life than one would ever guess from some of the sombre portraits of him, literary and photographic. 'All is well. All is well between us for ever and ever. . . . Remember.' His farewell to Helen places the significance and truth of his life in the setting of eternity. Poet, soldier, friend, lover, he found and finally expressed the same synthesis of human experience as the mediaeval anchoress Julian of Norwich had found. 'All shall be well, and all manner of thing shall be well.'

Epilogue

Jesse Berridge outlived his friend Edward Thomas by nearly half a century. He remained Rector of Little Baddow until his retirement in 1947 and became an honorary canon of Chelmsford in 1941. In that year he wrote to Rowland Watson: ' I have been here for 25 years and feel it is my job, so I suppose I should expect nothing very much better this side of death, – whatever that may be. I write little verses and sometimes puzzle my parishoners, but they put up with it, and me.' It seems a pity that he did not write his memoirs too, for his background and early life were strikingly different from what his parishioners probably assumed.

He was born at Milverton near Leamington on 4 April 1874, the second of the two children of Captain Henry Berridge, master mariner, and his wife Maud (née Timperley) who was a goddaughter of Sir Robert Peel. Jesse's brother Henry became a distinguished civil and military engineer who did important work on the Hudson Tunnel in New York, in Poole Harbour and at Plymouth; he was awarded the OBE for his services as Chief Engineer of Aden, developed housing schemes for the London County Council, was twice married, and died in 1946. The brothers were devoted to one another throughout their lives.

When Jesse was three, the family moved to London and lived for eleven years in Aubert Park, a handsome new terrace in Highbury. Captain Berridge was away at sea for months on end. On at least one voyage his wife and children sailed with him; at other times his wife accompanied him and the boys were left in the care of their maternal grandmother or were sent to stay with an uncle and aunt in Blackheath. It was on his father's last ship, the *Superb*, that the eight-year-old Jesse rounded Cape Horn and memorised the sea-shanties that he later contributed to one of Edward Thomas's anthologies. It is not known what formal education Harold and Jesse received in Highbury. After the family's next move (to Avenue Cresent, Acton, in 1888) they attended the City of London School for a term or two, leaving before they were sixteen. Captain Berridge had by then retired from the sea; if his affairs had prospered his sons would probably have stayed at school longer and gone on to university.

Captain Berridge's letters home leave an impression of a warm-hearted and devoutly Christian family man; they blend moral exhortation (for his sons) with enthusiastic description of Australian scenery. He is said to have bought a plot of land in Melbourne and it was unfortunate for his family that he did not keep it, since it later became part of one of the main streets of that city. He had been born at Melton Mowbray in Leicestershire, had gone to sea as a boy and become a master mariner before he was thirty. He commanded successively the *Clarence*, the *Walmer Castle*, the *High Flyer* and the *Superb*, all Blackwall clippers trading with the West and East Indies and later with Australia and San Francisco. The *Superb*, built in 1866, was one of the first iron three-masters, fast enough to be a favourite with passengers on the Australia run, though the voyage from Melbourne to Gravesend still took fourteen weeks in 1882. Captain Berridge's last voyage was in 1884; suffering from Bright's disease and diabetes, he needed a complete change after thirty years at sea. He invested his savings in a small private company dealing in mineral water, but had no experience of business and was ruined by the debts left by an absconding partner. He died in 1891 at the age of fifty-three. His wife Maud survived him until 1907.

Jesse was not quite seventeen when his father died, but he had already spent eighteen months in the London and South Western Bank where his mother's relatives had helped him to obtain a clerkship. Junior staff were expected to remain celibate, and when one day in 1895 the manager saw his employee in Piccadilly arm-in-arm with 'a raving bohemian beauty' he summoned him to his office for a fatherly lecture; the indignant young man flared up, announced that the lady was his wife and was duly dismissed. (For the next ten years he worked for the London agency of the Deutsche Bank in Lombard Street.) Jesse had indeed recently married Edna Adeline Dell, without the approval of his family too. She was a professional artist working for Raphael Tuck and Jesse is thought to have met her at the art school which he attended for a time. He evidently shared her progressive views (she was a member of the Fabian Society) for in later years he related the experience of being ducked in a Trafalgar Square fountain for demonstrating against his country's conduct of the South African war. The ensuing period of his life, that which is covered by the correspondence with Edward Thomas, has already been outlined in the Introduction to this volume. We move forward to 1916, the year in which the Reverend Jesse Berridge, now aged forty-one, took up his duties at Little Baddow.

Jesse Berridge in later life

Berridge had been a popular curate and he soon proved to be an enterprising country rector, liked and respected by his parishioners whether church-goers or not. Among his innovations were a monthly parish magazine (in which the 'little verses' he mentions appeared at the head of his pastoral letter), the sharing of Armistice Day services and Christmas carol-singing with the local Congregational church, and an annual Nativity play (written by himself). In Little Baddow church he uncovered the long-hidden fourteenth-century wall-painting of St Christopher, as well as the Norman north door, the stairs to the rood-loft, and the mediaeval beams of the nave roof. His antiquarian skill was not confined to his parish: he served on the council of the Essex Archaeological Society, helped to set up the county record office in Chelmsford and for twelve years acted as Cathedral Librarian.

Since the two books of sonnets of 1902 Berridge had published nothing, but when he was in his fifties his literary talent reappeared in a form which reflected his new interest in local history. He produced five novels, all set in mediaeval, Reformation or seventeenth-century Essex: *The Tudor Rose* (1925), *The Stronghold* (1926), *Brother John* (1927), *Gracys Walk* (1929) and *Bettina* (1933). The following year he published his *History of Little Baddow in the Seventeenth Century*. There was only one new volume of poetry, some religious verse entitled *Little Things*, which appeared in 1937.

Over this full and outwardly happy rural life, however, dark clouds had gathered early and were to cast their shadows over the succeeding years. Thirteen months after the loss of Berridge's dearest friend, and from the very same part of the Front, came news of the death of his eldest son. Dell had already been wounded twice and he had been awarded the Military Cross; he was killed near Arras on 24 May 1918. From this blow Edna Berridge never fully recovered; she withdrew from the life of the parish and became chronically ill; she died in 1945. Her three younger sons grew up at the Rectory and went from school to university. Denys became a housemaster at Epsom College; he died in 1979. Christian qualified as a solicitor, worked in local government, rose to become Clerk to the Essex County Council, and has now retired. Wilfrid taught Classics and became Senior Master at Maldon Grammar School; for a short period before his retirement he was Head of the new Lower Plume Comprehensive School. The descendants of Jesse and Edna Berridge, through their two youngest sons, now number three grandchildren and two great-grandchildren.

It is pleasant to record, in an epilogue to a collection of letters from Edward Thomas, that the friends he made in the Gray's Inn Road when he came down from Oxford kept in touch with each other and with his widow for the rest of their lives. Jesse Berridge and Helen Thomas exchanged letters every Christmas, and each of them remained in touch with Duncan and Margaret Williams (who had moved to Mill Hill in 1912). Helen, Jesse and Duncan met again at Steep on 2 October 1937 for the unveiling of the memorial sarsen stone on the Shoulder of Mutton hillside and of the plaque on Berryfield Cottage. The following year, Jesse and Duncan joined Franklin Dyall at the funeral of Charles Dalmon, who had died in the Charterhouse at the age of seventy-six. Duncan Williams had retired in 1933 from a senior post in the Comptroller's department of the London County Council; he had been the LCC chess champion, a great traveller who was widely read in several languages, a mountaineer and, to the end, an ardent Socialist; he died in 1963 at the age of ninety-one.

In 1957 Robert Frost visited England again. He had several meetings with Eleanor Farjeon, who put up Helen and Bronwen at her Hampstead cottage so that they could all go together to hear Frost lecture at London University. Eleanor wrote to tell Jesse Berridge about the occasion and enclosed a copy of her *London Magazine* article on Edward which became part of her book about him the following year (*Edward Thomas: the Last Four Years*). 'You will hear his voice in many of the letters in this article,' she wrote.

In a letter to Helen Thomas written in his late sixties, Berridge told her that he had been re-reading Edward's poems with even greater pleasure than before and finding more in them. He was delighted at their steadily increasing reputation and ready with his support for any form of tribute to his friend. In 1936 he had given the manuscript of *The Heart of England* to the memorial committee, writing to Rowland Watson, its inspirer, that he would be 'quite satisfied' if it found its home in the National Museum of Wales (see Letter 63). He never lost touch with Helen. 'We write spasmodically but the bond is unaffected by intervals of silence,' he told Watson. To all her family, too, he remained a much-loved friend. He baptised Bronwen and prepared her for confirmation at Little Baddow, and christened her son Charles at Chelsea Old Church. Myfanwy remembers him as an affectionate, gentle, humorous person, to whom the family went for comfort or rejoicing. 'We thought of Jesse as a saint, but a very earthly and human one, and we all felt a terrible sorrow when he died.'

Helen Thomas outlived her old friend by fourteen months. Since Edward's death she had lived in Otford, in Hampstead and near Chippenham, before settling for her last thirteen years at Eastbury in Berkshire. By the time of her death in her ninetieth year she had, to her great joy, three grandchildren and eight great-grandchildren. Her one sadness was the death of Mervyn shortly after his retirement in 1965 from a distinguished career as a technical journalist and editor in the field of motor transport. Bronwen died in 1975.

There are still people in Little Baddow who remember the old rector trudging round the parish with his stout walking-stick or bicycling (for he never drove a car) down the mile-long lane between the rectory and the church. He had an indomitable zest for life. In the early days he had enjoyed cricket and tennis and rough shooting; he was a good skater and a powerful swimmer. When he was a curate in Colchester he had been awarded a medal by the Royal Humane Society for rescuing a boy from the sea during an outing at Clacton, and in his own parish he saved a scout from drowning in the Chelmer. In the first world war he was a special constable, in the second an air raid warden. The story is still told of how the seventy-year-old canon climbed up a tall ladder to rescue a parishoner stranded in the bedroom of a bombed house – and carried her down on his back. His first head choirboy, who sang at the new rector's induction service in 1915, still lives in the village. For him, Jesse Berridge remains 'the most perfect man I have ever known'.

In 1947 Berridge retired from his parish to live in Colchester, where he and his second wife bought a semi-detached house in Canwick Grove. His marriage to Diana Beck had taken place the previous summer. She was the daughter of a London solicitor who lived in Little Baddow; the two families had been friends as well as neighbours for many years. As a Canon Emeritus of Chelmsford, Jesse Berridge continued to serve in the diocese for a few more years; he kept in touch with old friends, paid visits to his sons, went on writing little poems and complained only of the gradual loss of his eyesight. He died at the age of ninety-one, on 4 February 1966, and was buried close by the tower of his beloved church. Eighteen months later Diana Berridge was laid to rest in the same grave.

Some lines from Jesse Berridge's obituary in the *Essex Journal* may serve to conclude this account of his life. 'Many who knew and loved him well will recall happy memories of a devoted parish priest who served with compassion and common sense, a sound scholar whose writings were always illuminated with the gift of imagination, and a gentle, highly talented friend with a deep sense of humour.'

Works of Edward Thomas referred to in the Letters

(The year is that of first publication. Numbers of Letters follow the title in brackets. n. signifies an allusion in a note to the Letter.)

1897 The Woodland Life (5, 9)
1902 Horae Solitariae (8, 11, 13, 15n, 24, 50)
1903 The Poems of John Dyer (edited by ET) (21)
1903 Oxford (19n, 26, 27)
1905 Beautiful Wales (30, 31)
1906 The Heart of England (27n, 37, 63)
1907 The Pocket Book of Poems and Songs for the Open Air (36, 37, 38)
1907 The Book of the Open Air (edited by ET) (36, 37)
1909 Richard Jefferies (39-46, 49)
1909 The South Country (48, 49)
1910 Rest and Unrest (50)
1910 Feminine Influence on the Poets (33n, 51-55)
1911 Maurice Maeterlinck (51, 54, 56)
1912 Norse Tales (59, 60)
1912 Algernon Charles Swinburne (60)
1912 George Borrow (48, 49)
1913 The Icknield Way (42n, 57)
1913 The Country (64n)
1913 The Happy-Go-Lucky Morgans (63n)
1913 Walter Pater (57-60)
1914 In Pursuit of Spring (62n, 63, 66)
1915 The Life of the Duke of Marlborough (69)
1917 A Literary Pilgrim in England (66)
1922 Cloud Castle (50n)
1928 The Last Sheaf (67n)
1938 The Childhood of Edward Thomas (65)
     also various unnamed poems (68, 69, 70)